POLISH POLITICS AND NATIONAL REFORM
1775-1788

DANIEL STONE

EAST EUROPEAN QUARTERLY, BOULDER
DISTRIBUTED BY COLUMBIA UNIVERSITY PRESS
NEW YORK

1976

EAST EUROPEAN MONOGRAPHS, NO. XXII

Daniel Stone is Associate Professor of History
at the University of Winnipeg

ACKNOWLEDGEMENTS

This book is a revised and heavily abridged version of my doctoral dissertation. I gratefully acknowledge the advice and detailed criticism of my advisor, Professor Herbert Kaplan, as well as the careful attention and useful observations of Professor Charles Jelavich, Professor Gerald Strauss, and the late Professor Vaclav Beneš. I should also like to express my thanks to Professor Andrzej Zahorski, whose seminar at Warsaw University I attended at various times, and the many other Polish scholars who gave their time generously to help an inexperienced foreigner. The archivists and librarians were more helpful than can be described.

I also acknowledge appreciately financial aid. The bulk of the research and writing was financed by a fellowship from the Foreign Area Fellowship Program. A grant from the University of Winnipeg research fund assisted me in the final stages and in manuscript preparation.

TABLE OF CONTENTS

CHAPTER I

INTRODUCTION

THE MOVEMENT FOR NATIONAL REFORM

During early modern times, most of Europe's larger states attempted to set up bureaucratic structures to assure internal stability and external power, but the Polish-Lithuanian Republic fell into an abject state of political, economic, and cultural decline. The wars and repeated invasions of the mid-seventeenth century made Polish weakness perfectly obvious to the rest of Europe. Politically, a unique constitution paralyzed the central government by stripping the king of most of his power on behalf of a diet which itself ceased functioning effectively. Economically, the noble landowners oppressed their serfs and destroyed the prosperity of cities. Isolated and backward, Poland failed to move with the mainstream of European cultural development and lingered over the classical heritage of the Baroque Counter-Reformation.

Paradoxically, most Polish nobles felt a "sense of national power, greatness, and inexhaustible strength."(1) They believed Poland to be the best state in Europe. Picturesquely dressed in long caftans, sporting moustaches, and shaving their heads Turkish-style, the Polish nobles of the late seventeenth and early eighteenth centuries developed a unique style of life, an exotic variant of the European Baroque. Equality, Catholicism, and agrarianism were among their fundamental values. Equality stemmed from fancied common "racial" origins of Polish nobles in the ancient Sarmatian people; it found expression in proverbs and in the use of informal address in speech. Catholicism became an integral part of this concept of Polish nationality through the constant seventeenth-century wars against Turkish Moslems, Russian Orthodox Christians, and Swedish or German Protestants. Except when called to the defense of the nation, the Polish noble considered himself profoundly pacifistic, preferring to spend his life on his landed estate while benevolently supervising the work of his serfs. "Sarmatian" nobles used politics to realize their ideals and succeeded in building a political system which acted as a vehicle for their desires. They remained oblivious to its failings since the least change in it appeared to threaten their entire way of life.

Under the Polish constitution, each noble could participate in provincial dietines which elected deputies to the central diet. In the lower chamber, elaborate procedural guarantees protected individual self-expression. Individual sovereignty was safeguarded by the unanimity rule in voting. This practice grew without specific legislative sanction until it became the *liberum veto* by which a single deputy could "explode" the entire session of the diet by saying *nie pozwalam* (I do not permit), nullifying all previous legislation and preventing the diet from sitting again. A veto could even be cast before the diet ever met. An upper chamber, or Senate, consisting of bishops and high civil authorities also had to approve decisions unanimously. Diets met ordinarily for six weeks every second year; "extraordinary" diets called at other times operated under the same cumbersome procedures.

To assure some kind of government in times of crisis, nobles banded together in "confederations" which took precedence over the normal conduct of affairs. Diets and dietines could meet as confederations so that the *liberum veto* would not apply and decisions would be reached by a simple majority vote. As the governmental crisis reached its depths in the first half of the eighteenth century, no "free" diet (as non-confederated diets were called) succeeded in reaching its natural term. Only confederated diets added any legislation to the law books.

Despite legal equality, the nobility divided economically in three parts. First, a thin crust of fabulously rich magnates dominated Polish politics. Families like the Radziwiłłs, Potockis, Czartoryskis, Sanguszkos, and Sapiehas owned thousands of villages with tens or even hundreds of thousands of inhabitants and enjoyed incomes comparable to European monarchs. Traditionally, these families translated wealth into political power by retaining the services of a second group, poor nobles whose poverty was so extreme that some went barefoot and farmed the land themselves. Since the noble identity gave these retainers the legal right to carry swords, they provided the armed force for magnates to control local dietines and, if educated, served as administrators, lawyers, or even deputies to the diet. In order to maintain their noble status, the poorer nobility enthusiastically supported traditional political practices. A third group of nobles in the middle enjoyed moderate wealth drawn from feudal ownership of several villages. Rich enough to support themselves comfortably and occupy some independent position in the state, these nobles could not aspire to independent leadership during Sarmatian times.

A relative handful of nobles in the beginning of the eighteenth century (increasing numerically in later years) recognized the need to rejuvenate Poland. Reform projects designed to provide more effective government by strengthening the diet were advanced as early as 1673. The overwhelming majority of reformers were republicans, who drew on native traditions to advocate parliamentary superiority, or even supremacy, over the king as well as the revitalization of the diet through restriction or abolition of the *liberum veto*. The creation of a collegial authority composed of members of the diet which would exercise executive authority was frequently advocated to this end. The leading voice of reform, Piarist Father Stanisław Konarski, compared the Polish Republic to ''an old and great ship which had been completely neglected or only patched and which would be destroyed if not fundamentally overhauled''.(2) A minor key in reform cane from the monarchs, especially August II and Stanisław August Poniatowski, who wished to enlarge their own prerogatives and introduce reforms which would allow them to play a more significant role in European politics.

The development of the Enlightenment in Polish culture added new perceptions to old problems. A contemporary observer noted that Enlightenment culture began to spread to Poland around 1700 when great lords, travelling to Dresden to attend the court, brought back novelties in fashion.(3) By the 1760's, the entire upper nobility and sections of both the lesser nobility and bourgeoisie had adopted Western dress, learned the French language, acquired at least a nodding familiarity with the *philosophes,* and displayed the trappings of Enlightened style. Warsaw grew rapidly at this time. It came to resemble other European capitals so that the English traveller, Nathaniel Wraxall, who visited it in 1778, found within it ''the entire refinement of Paris, art of Florence, and luxury of Petersburg''. He noted that western clothing styles dominated to such an extent that ''a visitor in Polish costume would look like . . . a foreigner''.(4) Outside Warsaw, more traditional styles maintained themselves, but they were losing ground rapidly, especially around the country residences of the magnates.

While the Enlightenment provided cultural changes, it also provided a new standard by which to measure Polish society. In the more serious aspects of Enlightenment culture, society was often examined critically. Magazines like *Monitor* (1765-84), modelled after the English *Spectator,* gave advice on everything from social manners to philosophy. The editor, Father Franciszek Bohomolec, who wrote much of what was published, combatted uncritical traditionalism energetically; mindless imitations of foreign ways also drew his fire. Throughout most of the 1770's and 1780's, the king organized a kind of royal academy of arts and sciences which met regularly for Thursday Dinner after which serious discussions took place. Much of the attention of the group was turned to poetry and the monthly journal *Pleasant and Useful Amusements (Zabawy przyjemne i pozyteczne)* acted as a house organ from 1770 to 1777 when the king asked the editor, Bishop Adam Naruszewicz, to write a history of Poland. Naruszewicz produced six volumes in the next ten years covering Polish history to 1366. His history interpreted the past through the eyes of the present. He declared that the prime causes of domestic disorder had been "the pride of the magnates, interregna, and the election of kings".(5) Father Piotr Świtkowski's *Historico-Political and Economic Journal (Pamietnik Historyczno-Polityczny, Ekonomiczny)* ran from 1782 until its suppression by the Targowica government in 1792. This impressive journal printing some eighty pages of long articles per issue advocated a wide variety of political, economic, and social reforms.

The outstanding poet of the age, Ignacy Krasicki, Bishop of Warmia, gained his first fame through his "Hymn to Patriotism" written for the Royal Cadet School. The *Fables* and *Lyrics* brought him much attention. Later, Krasicki wrote two long heroicomic epics, *Myszeidos* (The Epic of the Mice) which satirized baroque poetry and Sarmatian Chronicles and *Monomachia* (The War of the Monks), which poked fun at monastic superstition. Krasicki also wrote prose, A picaresque novel, *Mikołaj Doswiadczyński Przypadki* (The Adventures of Nicholas Find-Out) presented a young noble, spoiled by his French tutor, who eventually learns true virtue from exotic philosophers in a strange land. In a kind of sequel, *Pan Podstoli* (The Squire), Krasicki depicted an ideal noble who lives in his estates, cultivated his garden, and cared for the welfare of his serfs.

Theatre discussed society, too. As an anonymous contributor to the *Journal litteraire de Varsovie* commented, "good comedy is needed in Poland . . . You can correct men's faults easiest while making them laugh".(6) During the 1760's, Father Franciszek Bohomolec and Prince Adam Czartoryski wrote plays for school use which were designed to poke fun at Sarmatian traditionalists. The creation of a public theatre after the first partition allowed the rapid production of current plays from the west as well as local works. The leading Polish playwright was Franciszek Zabłocki, a poor noble who turned out fifty-four dramas in the 1780's, most of them translations or adaptations. *Sarmatyzm* caricatured two landowners as crude, ignorant persons who spend all their time quarelling pointlessly and *Zabobonnik* (The Superstitious Man) rounded out the portrait by castigating belief in omens. *Fircyk w Zalotach* (The Fop-Suitor), however, attacked the excesses of a Frenchified dandy. "Bourgeois drama" also began to appear on the stage with its complement of middle-class and peasant heroes.

The movement for political reform and the Enlightenment went hand-in-hand in the field of education. The movement for educational reform began with Stanisław Leszczyński, the would-be king of Poland, whose Knights' Academy in Nancy taught natural science, history, modern languages, manners, and the art of war. Father Stanisław Konarski, one of Leszczyński's supporters, brought a version of the program to Poland to replace the Latinate curriculum which prevailed there, first in his own *Collegium Nobilium* and after his appointment as Visitor to all the Piarist schools in Poland, throughout the country, Polish became a language of instruction and courses in Polish language, history, geography, law, and literature were introduced. Debates on Poland's current problems even took place. The Jesuits, who ran more than two-thirds of all the schools in Poland, soon imitated Konarski's reforms and went much further studying natural science. The activities of these two orders underline the great contributions made by the clergy to the Polish Enlightenment.

After his coronation in 1764, King Stanisław August Poniatowski set up a Royal Cadet School which offered a comprehensive curriculum particularly rich in modern languages. Many of the instructors were foreigners. Prince Adam Czartoryski, the king's cousin, became commander-in-chief and used his private income to buy equipment for the school. The Cadet School made a special effort to implant moral and patriotic principles in its students through the teaching of "love of country, the rules of honor, and hatred for all shameful acts."(7) Graduates played a prominent role in the Kościuszko Uprising, the Polish Legions, and the 1830 Insurrection.

The abolition of the Jesuit Order in 1773 threatened to close the vast majority of Polish schools for lack of staff and funding. Poles responded with rare unanimity as all factions recognized that "it is the republican form of government which needs education the most."(8) The Jesuit estates were liquidated to provide the funds for the new schools, but there was so much corruption that their value was reduced immensely. A new National Education Commission composed of the king and prominent nobles worked honestly and effectively to administer what was left. Membership on the Commission included the king's relatives as well as prominent members of the Opposition. Both political camps worked together without discord. The curriculum essentially the same as the reformed Jesuit schools, was drawn up by a board of professional educators, including a number of ex-Jesuits. New textbooks were written. Overall, the Commission schools carried on existing trends with some innovation, but this was no mean accomplishment under the circumstances.

Textbooks fundamentally criticized the Sarmatian traditions of government. Father Antoni Popławski's *Collection of Diverse Political Matters* (1774) demanded the extension of royal courts to peasants and recognition of their property rights. He desired the creation of an hereditary monarchy and the abolition of the *Liberum veto*. Its replacement, Father Hieronim Stroynowski's *Course of Natural Law, Political Law, Political Economy, and International Law* (1785) was a more systematic text. Father Wincenty Skrzetuski addressed himself to politics directly in two volumes written for the Royal Cadet School. Skrzetuski praised the reforms of the 1760's and 1770's, and called for the abolition of the *liberum veto,* emancipation of the serfs (after suitable educational preparation), and enfranchisement of the bourgeoisie in the royal cities. The two most famous treatises on political reform, Father Stanislaw Staszic's *Observations on the Life of Jan Zamoyski* and Father Hugo Kollataj's *Anonymous Letters* were written on the eve of the Four Year Diet and belong to that period.

Economics were also affected by the new winds sweeping Poland. Regardless of their politics, many nobles on their estates carried out reforms which ranged from the switching of peasant obligations from labor dues to monetary rent and the founding of manufactures to simple technical improvements in methods of cultivation. Although serfdom was scarcely touched as an institution, public discussion began with the academic authors and the controversy surrounding the Zamoyski Law Code. In his *Patriotic Letters* (1777). Jozef Wybicki argued that free labor was more productive and therefore profitable than serf labor. Some landowners switched their serfs from labor dues to cash rent for a mixture of humanitarian and profit-seeking motives. The reforms succeeded where nearby markets permitted the peasants to sell their produce and earn the cash required. The late 1760's and early 1770's saw hard times because of the civil war of the Bar Confederation and the partitions, but prosperity returned with years of peace. Although exports of grain were severely hampered by Prussian restrictions of Polish trade along the Vistula, a favorable balance of trade was achieved by 1784. Alternate trade routes through Riga and Cherson were developed. Nobles also sponsored urban settlements on their estates, frequently nearby or even within existing cities. Such settlements generally developed with autonomous civil government established under Magdeburg or Chełm law. Many German Protestants came to Poland as well as smaller numbers of other nationalities.

The same mixture of patriotic and financial reasons brought an increase in domestic manufactures. Poland was never totally unindustrialized. Home production and village crafts satisfied most peasant needs in the early eighteenth century. South-central Poland supplied about 85% of Poland's iron and steel requirements despite foreign competition. The textile industry of Wielkopolska also had national significance.

A number of magnates turned to manufacturing after 1740 and set up factories on their estates to produced luxury goods which sold generally in the local area, especially to dependent nobles and burghers. Technicians were imported from abroad for skilled tasks while free labor, often vagabonds, were recuited for the remaining jobs. Serfs were used only for construction of buildings. Low quality production restricted the circulation of goods but they successfully maintained a more favorable "balance of payments" for the magnate manufacturer, himself, and eventually, for Poland as a whole. Food processing and construction industries established around urban centers by nobles, burghers, clerics, and Jews prospered.

Among the most notable private manufactures were the mint, cannon foundry, and small arms factory established by King Stanisław August. Poniatowski's political lieutenant in Lithuania, Vice-Treasurer Antoni Tyzenhauz, established twenty-three factories employing 3,000 workers at Grodno, but the enormous complex was overextended and poorly managed. It could be kept going only with continual subsidies. When these were cut off for political reasons, most factories closed. Jacek Jezierski, Castellan of Łuków, was more successful. He started a luxury brothel in the suburbs of Warsaw, turned the profits into a salt extracting company, and ended with a company producing agricultural implements.

In order to improve trade, the long-neglected Polish cities were cleaned up and put on a firmer financial footing by Commissions of Good Order. Composed of nobles, the Commission worked closely, although not always harmoniously, with the local burghers. Cooperation between the two estates carried over into several joint stock companies created in the 1760's, 1770's, and 1780's. Encouraged from above, the burghers gained self-confidence and appealed constantly to the diet and ministers for confirmation and expansion of monopolistic trade privileges. Such privileges generally came at the expense of the most dynamic elements of the Polish urban economy: Jewish, noble, and clerical enterprise. Of greater short-term significance than the growing visibility of the burghers was the emergence of new elements from the lesser nobility like Jacek Jezierski, Antoni Tyzenhauz, or Stanisław August Poniatowski himself. These new men gained national prominence often through advocacy of greater trade, industrialization, and urbanization or through actual involvement in business activities.

While at least the winds of change were moving through most areas of Polish life, politics remained little affected. The Polish constitution granted the king less power than other European monarchs. Elected for life by the nobility, he yielded control of taxation and military affairs to the diet. Foreign affairs, technically in the hands of the king, were really dominated by the diet which had to approve all treaties unanimously. A number of ministerial posts existed, theoretically to assist the king in the conduct of affairs, but with life tenure, gave the ministers the power to act independently of both diet and king. Justice, normally an area of royal concern in Europe, was generally conducted by the nobility in elected provincial tribunals. Royal assessorial courts judged only the burghers and peasants of the royal domains. Even in the capital itself, an independent minister meted out justice. Despite extreme weakness, the Polish kings often succeeded in playing leading roles in politics as leaders of political factions, or "parties" in eighteenth century terminology. Through patronage in high church and civil posts as well as through granting orders, pensions, and positions in the royal household, the kings gained supporters who did their bidding in dietines and the national diet.

With Poland undergoing transformation, it was logical that at least one of the many magnate families struggling for political power would become identified with the cause of reform. August and Michał Czartoryski, supported by a powerful political faction based on family relations, developed a program for governmental efficiency whereby the *liberum veto* would be abolished and the diet would gain greater superiority over the king than it already possessed. A cabinet-type government, composed of members of the diet and responsible to it, would replace the king as supreme executive authority. Too weak to gain control of the Republic by themselves after the death of King August III in 1763, the Czartoryskis formed an alliance with Russia which sent troops to install Stanislaw (August) Poniatowski, nephew of the Czartoryskis and former lover of Empress Catherine II, on the Polish throne. The Czartoryskis confidently expected to guide their nephew in all matters, keeping real power in their own hands. They enacted part of their program at the diet of 1764.

Stanisław Poniatowski, who took the sobriquet "August" at coronation, came to the throne in 1764 determined to rule as well as to reign. A careful education and personal observation during a grand tour of Western Europe brought him to the conclusion that Poland had to reconcile political liberty with executive power (and) fight against oligarchy and anarchy". He intended to make Poland "a modern state endowed with an English-style constitution".(9) As king, Poniatowski used all the usual political techniques to build a party loyal to himself alone. Instead of granting favors only to members of the Czartoryski party, he also enlisted "new men", nobles of mediocre fortune whose lives would have been spent in provincial obscurity if not for their service to the king. These included a number of foreigners, mostly Italians and Swiss. Poniatowski was handicapped in his search for political power, however, by a lack of personal fortune. The king's father had worked his way into the upper nobility through military and diplomatic accomplishments, but did not leave wealth comparable to that possessed by older families like the Potockis, Czartoryskis, or Radziwiłłs.

Stanisław August worked extremely hard as king. His education gave him a good grasp of politics, economics, education, and philosophy. He had one quality uncommon in Poland at that time, the patience to administer a system on a day-to-day basis. The volume of his correspondence at home and abroad, on matters as diverse as literature, statecraft, and the personal problems of his subjects testifies to his energy and extraordinary mastery of detail. The king lost no opportunity to placate enemies, entice neutral parties, and encourage his supporters.

The flaw in this picture of a master politician is that Poniatowski lacked the strong will which might have enabled him to realize his vision. At each of the numerous crises of his reign, he yielded to pressure and resigned himself to the loss of all he had accomplished rather than provide an heroic example. Foreign observers sensed the problem. Louis-Philippe Ségur, French ambassador to Russia in the 1780's, cuttingly noted after a short visit to Warsaw that the king's father had "wanted to make an austere sage and statesman of him; he only became a well-read *littérateur,* a lively courtier, an agreeable speaker, and a brilliant cavalier".(10) Poles complained about their king's lack of martial virtues. On the occasion of the unveiling of a statue commemorating the hundredth anniversary of Sobieski's relief of Vienna, a Polish satirist wrote:

Sto tysięcy na pomnik! Ja by dwakroć łożył
Gdyby Staś był skamieniał a Jan Trzeci ożył.

''One hundred thousand for a monument! I would give twice as much if Stanisław turned to stone and Jan III returned to life''(11)

Poniatowski's policies won him independent strength at the price of antagonizing much of the nobility. Traditionalist, Sarmatian nobles feared possible absolutist designs, particularly through the influence of Italian advisers. The king's cosmopolitanism confirmed their worst fears while his abstemious habits bitterly offended them. His former protectors, the Czartoryskis, also turned away, angered that they were deprived of the fruits of their victory.

In isolation, the king found himself at the mercy of the Russians, who failed to follow a consistent policy to achieve their aim of making Poland a useful, but subordinate, ally. The 1764 diet, which met as a confederation, enacted Czartoryski sponsored reforms restricting the *liberum veto* to ''matters of state'' (as opposed to ''economic matters'' which passed by majority vote) and creating military and treasury commissions elected by the diet. But Russia came to fear that effective reform would strengthen Poland excessively so the ambassador, Count Nikolai Repnin, allied himself with anti-Czartoryski forces of a ''Sarmatian'' mentality at the 1766 diet to dissolve the confederation. Demands on the part of Russia and Prussia for the enfranchisement Protestant and Orthodox Polish nobles, the ''Dissidents'', brought further confusion to the political scene. At the 1768 diet, Russia pleased the Sarmatians by forcing enactment of the Fundamental Laws which cut off all hope of further political reform, although it did maintain the legislation of 1764-5, but she enraged them by deporting leaders of the patriotic Catholic party which opposed concessions to the Dissidents. A guerilla war broke out as members of a confederation formed in the town of Bar sought to expel the Russians from Poland and in 1771, tried to depose Poniatowski because he would not break with Russia. Skirmishes between Russians and Confederates on Poland's southeastern border led to the outbreak of war between Turkey and Russia. In the confusion, Austria unilaterally occupied several Polish districts to which she had a flimsy claim, thereby setting a precedent for partition. In the first partition, Poland lost approximately one-third her population and territory.

This disaster marked the beginning of total Polish dependence on Russia. While Prussia and Austrian armies restricted their activies to areas seized in the partition, Russian troops occupied the entire country, including Warsaw. A diet summoned to ratify the partition met under the domination of the Russian ambassador. Polish defiance expressed itself in a few dramatic gestures but no effective political or military resistance could be mounted. The king alone found means to delay ratification until concessions were offered.

Russia's aims were not entirely inimical to Poland. The Empress Catherine had not really wanted to partition Poland; she preferred to rule it all as a vassal. Russian leaders blamed anarchic conditions in Poland for creating the disorder which led to Austrian and Prussian involvement and resolved to establish an effective government that would keep Poland peaceful. Thus, the partition Diet, which met from 1773 to 1775, enacted both harmful and useful measures. On the one hand, it granted legal recognition to the partition. On the other hand, it enacted some reforms. A sign of growing reformist spirit was passage by the diet of a law permitting nobles to take part in commerce without losing their rank. A number of other measures concerning freer trade and the improvement of peasant conditions somewhat were advanced by failed.

The most important acts were those creating the National Education Commission and the Permanent Council. The latter was composed of thirty-six members of the diet, eighteen from each chamber. It met both as a full council and as five separate "departments": military, treasury, foreign affairs, justice, and police. The king acted as chairman and retained certain patronage rights, but decisions reached by majority vote were final.

While the diet reached its height of power in theory, royal government reached its apex in practice. Political alliance with Russia enabled Poniatowski to dominate elections to the diet and to the Permanent Council. Since the diet met only every second year and since the Council developed no independent policy, the king carried on much of his activities outside the official government. A "cabinet" which employed at its height in 1779 thirty-four persons carried on his private correspondence. Polish diplomats (most important of which was Antoni Deboli in St. Petersburg) generally sent fuller dispatches to him than to the Permanent Council. A separate military chancellory under the direction of General Jan Komarzewski effectively modernized the slender Polish army through the implementation of Prussian-style drill and adequate technical services. Neither the king nor the diet put much money into the army, though. It remained almost 50% under the 30,000 troops allowed by treaty.

Magnus Stackelberg, the Russian ambassador, kept Poland under close supervision. Before coming to Warsaw, he had served as Russian minister to Spain, where he took good advantage of his proximity to France by schooling himself in French manners and wit. As a result,

Stackelberg appeared unusually polite, controlled, and especially pleasing to women. His finesse and subtlety in dealings with Stanislaw August led the king to exclaim that the ambassador "tyrannized (over him) in a most piquant fashion."(12)

The ambassador met frequently, almost daily, with the king and insisted on knowing the business of the day, even inspecting Polish diplomatic correspondence. The ambassador extended his influence to the details of the king's personal life, selecting domestics, artists, and inviting guests to the royal palace without permission. Combining political and social supremacy, Stackelberg cut a more royal figure in the Polish capital than the king. When the newly-appointed Austrian ambassador, Baron Karol Thugut, came for his first audience, he saw an elaborately dressed figure surrounded by courtiers. Taking him for the king, Thugut approached and made the customary three deep bows. He was extremely embarrassed when Stanislaw August came over from a side alcove and introduced himself.(13)

Although the Polish king himself compared Stackelberg to a Roman Proconsul ruling over satellite nations in the ancient world, the king was not without political weapons. Catherine had given her ambassador a difficult assignment. Russian troops could not be used to administer Poland for diplomatic and financial reasons, and Stackelberg needed suitable Polish agents who had sufficient resources to keep Poland peaceful, yet would still remain subservient to his will. Alliance with traditionalist nobles could scarcely work since they desired precisely those anarchic constitutional provisions which had opened the door in the past to foreign intervention. In 1774, Stackelberg decided to ally himself with Stanisław August.

The king enthusiastically accepted Stackelberg's overtures. He became Russia's prime agent in the hope of coopting her. When his own strength was lacking, he could now turn to Russian troops to suppress opposition or tap Russian funds for his political activities. The results of this policy pleased the king, who wrote in his memoirs that Stackelberg had "rendered (Poland) real services" whatever his motives had been.(14) Although the ambassador's airs infuriated him, Poniatowski gave way to requests without trickery. He was motivated by the knowledge that Stackelberg was too astute to be fooled for long. Besides, Poniatowski always hoped that Russia would permit further reform.

Many Polish nobles resented the king's new-found strength. Continuing the centuries-old battle of republicans against royalists, the great families banded together for united action into a group known variously as the Opposition, the Magnate Party, and the Ministerial Party. Like the king, the Opposition recognized that Russia would continue to dominate Poland so they aimed simply at replacing Stanisław August as Russia's agent. Nobles within the Opposition represented a variety of points of view from Sarmatian ideologists to highly cultured perveyors of the Enlightenment and from reactionary politicians to republican reformers. The major part of the parliamentary Opposition came from the Czartoryski Party which subordinated state policy ideals to the achievement of power. Failing to gain power through reform in the 1760's, it turned to reaction in the 1770's in the hope of winning wide public support. Even though its members personally shared the king's cultural program and cooperated fully with him on the National Education Commission as well as other non-political reform institutions, it appealed to those Polish nobles who were dissatisfied with the new ideas and fashions which the king sponsored.

The modernization of Poland demanded political reform. This depended on Russian permission, which clearly would not extend to fundamental issues. However, useful minor economic and administrative adjustments were possible if the two rival groups could become sufficiently reconciled in view of the dangers surrounding Poland in the partition era to pass them. Reconciliation might have more far-reaching effects, too. If Russian control over Poland ever collapsed, the opportunity would arise for the achievement of genuine independence.

CHAPTER II

STRENGTHENING THE PERMANENT COUNCIL

The first partition of Poland came as a blow to that part of Russian opinion which desired to maintain Polish territorial integrity in order to control it all. The partition had been forced on Catherine by events, though she put up little resistance, Ambassador Magnus Stackelberg, sent to Poland in 1773 by the Russian Government, made it his policy to prevent further internal disorder so that the neighboring powers would have no excuse to intervene again. He intended to strengthen the central government and introduce sound administrative practices by reducing the influence of the king and the powerful, independent ministers.(1) In conjunction with Nikita Panin, President of the Russian College of Foreign Affairs, Stackelberg worked over plans to alter the Polish constitution through the establishment of a collegiate form of government. Russian plans fitted in well with Polish political thought. For over seventy years, reformers had been urging creation of a governing body chosen by the diet which would rule Poland in the long intervals between meetings of the diet. These plans foresaw the growth of legislative authority at the expense of the already weak Polish king.(2)

Stackelberg put these plans into effect at the 1773-1775 diet by creating the Permanent Council. To force the diet to enact legislation setting up the Council and ratify the partition, the Russian ambassador relied heavily on certain Polish allies, mercenary types from the lower and middle socio-economic ranks of the nobility, who became known as the Russian party. One of these, August Sułkowski, Prince of the Holy Roman Empire and Palatin of Gniezno, had already approached the Russian government with ideas for stripping the Polish king of his royal powers and bestowing them on the diet. Adam Poniński, Great Crown Treasurer, also contributed his ideas but was better known as head of the parliamentary "Delegation" which ruled Poland dictatorially between 1773-1775. Other members, included Bishop Adam Młodziejowski (Crown Chancellor), Tomasz Gurowski (Lithuanian Court Marshal), Bishop Tomasz Ostrowski (Primate of the Polish Church), Bishop Adam Krasiński, and the king's brother, Kazimierz Poniatowski. All gained substantial wealth from their association with the Russians.(3)

Stackelberg ruled Poland from 1773 to 1775 through force or the threat of force from Russian troops occupying Poland but he hoped to return to strictly political means thereafter. To broaden the base of Russian political support in Poland, the ambassador turned to Stanisław August whose ''Royal Party'' promised an effective means of controlling diets, dietines, and tribunals. Stackelberg formed a political alliance with the Polish king by offering legislative concessions enabling Stanisław August to rule through the Permanent Council. Russian support permitted Poniatowski to dispense patronage and enlarge the Royal Party. Members of Stackelberg's original Russian Party continued to serve the ambassador but they also had to come to terms with the king.(4)

The alliance between King Stanisław August and Russian ambassador Stackelberg aimed at providing a stable Polish government adhering firmly to Russia. It was cemented by the Permanent Council which became an instrument of royal policy despite its anti-royalist origins. Security was provided through a formal guarantee by Russia, Prussia, and Austria ''of each and every constitution (law) made by the diet . . . concerning the form of free and independent republican government.''(5) The guarantee warned Poles that they could not try to alter the Permanent Council without risking reprisals. Nor could they hope to play the powers off against each other.

With the king and the ambassador pursuing a common course, the independent ministers found themselves the only ones whose real power had been reduced by the creation of the Permanent Council. Understandably angered at their decline, these ministers opposed the king and the Council so consistently that they became known simply as the Opposition. The high price of buying ministerial posts as well as tradition limited the occupancy of these posts to the richest families of the Republic.(6) Most of the Opposition, therefore, consisted of Polish magnates or their allies giving the Opposition the names of Ministerial Party and Magnate Party.(7)

Since most members of the Opposition were members of the Czartoryski family either by blood or marriage, the Russian party of 1764, they continued the republican program of the old Czartoryski Party without, however, adapting it to the new circumstances. Michał Czartoryski died in 1775 at the age of seventy-nine and his twin brother, August, lived on until 1782 in semi-retirement. Prince Adam Kazimierz Czartoryski, August's son, proved a great disappointment to his father and uncle by generally preferring a literary and pedagogical life to constant political activity. In 1764, Prince Adam even refused to become a candidate for the Polish throne.(8) This powerful political faction continued after 1775 under the leadership of August's son-in-law, Stanisław Lubomirski, Crown Great Marshal.

Ambitious and vindictive while subtle and well-informed, Stanisław Lubomirski desired to maintain the full prerogatives of his ministerial post. Lubomirski strengthened his personal position by effecting the union of two of the greatest families of Poland, the Potockis and the Czartoryskis, whose feuds had overshadowed all political developments in the first half of the eighteenth century. Ignacy Poocki, Stanisław Kostka Potocki, and Jan Potocki all married the Marshal's daughters, gradndaughters of August Czartoryski. Another of Lubomirski's sons-in-law, Crown Field General Seweryn Rzewuski hated the Russians and Stanisław August because of his arrest and exile to Siberia in 1768. Michał Ogiński, Lithuanian Great General, was married to Aleksandra Czartoryska, daughter of Michał Czartoryski. Although he was more interested in art than in politics, Ogiński nevertheless contributed political services to the Opposition.(9)

Political action against the Permanent Council and the king was initiated by Franciszek Xawery Branicki, Crown Great General. Alone of the Opposition, Branicki had been born in relative obscurity and owed his rise to service with Stanisław August. The king sent Branicki on a number of important political missions and appointed him Crown Great General, giving him an exaggerated idea of his abilities and importance. In 1774, Branicki represented the Polish diet and the king in Petersburg arguing against the establishment of the Permanent Council which would restrict his new powers as minister as well as the king's. Branicki failed to persuade the Russian Court to drop its plans for reorganizing the Polish government, but he gained a personal success. Empress Catherine II granted him valuable presents since her favorite, Grigorii Potemkin, was personally very attracted to him.(10) Stanisław August supported Branicki's plan to make the ministers permanent members of the Permanent Council at first, but when the king joined forces with Stackelberg and abandoned the ministers, Branicki joined the Opposition. His current mistress, Adam Czartoryski's wife, encouraged Branicki to support her brother, Stanisław Lubomirski, in action against the king. Morals were such that the affair led to no estrangement between Prince Adam and Branicki.(11)

At the conclusion of the 1775 diet, Branicki and Adam Czartoryski set off for Petersburg on their own authority in the hope of becoming Russia's primary agents for Poland. Catherine received Branicki very well, allowing him a place in the celebrations over the peace treaty with

Turkey, inviting him to her summer residence, and giving him valuable presents including the promise of 30,000 rifles for the Polish army. Potemkin continued to be very friendly. He promised to use his influence as President of the War College to evacuate Russian troops so that Branicki could dominate Poland as commander of the army. With this encouragement, the Polish Hetman (general and minister) spoke freely in public of the need for Russia to shed her alliance with Prussia and Austria so as to control all Poland through the ministers. By the time he left Petersburg in the early fall of 1775, Branicki thought he had succeeded. But Branicki misjudged the situation badly. His anti-Prussian policy alienated Panin who still dominated Russian foreign policy and who continued to support ambassador Stackelberg's system of cooperation with Stanisław August. Panin blocked the evacuation of Russian troops from Poland at this time.(12)

Members of the Opposition met with Branicki and Czartoryski on their return to Poland to make plans for a political offensive. Branicki cheered them by announcing that he had achieved a great success in Petersburg which would result in the evacuation of Russian troops from Poland and the calling of an extraordinary diet to enact constitutional changes. News of Russian troop movements in the provinces seem to confirm Branicki's account.(13)

The Russian Party in Poland began to fear that it would be abandoned by the Russian court. August Sułkowski, Marshal of the Permanent Council, warned Stackelberg that the Opposition intended to abolish the Permanent Council if Russian troops left. Alarmed, Stackelberg sent a courier to Petersburg to investigate whether evacuation were indeed intended. After three weeks, the courier returned with assurance that enough troops would remain in Poland to assure the Russian ambassador's control over Poland. Rumors of evacuation continued for several weeks until it became obvious that the troops had simply moved into winter quarters within the Polish-Lithuanian state. Stackelberg was finally able to assure Chancellor Adam Młodziejowski in late November that Russian troops would not leave Poland and that Russia would not abandon her support of the present Polish government.(14)

The Opposition remained determined to undermine the authority of the Permanent Council by taking advantage of inconsistencies in the legislation establishing the Council. The 1775 diet had created the Council without abolishing or altering significantly the statutory powers of the ministers and the governing commissions. Branicki acted first. Since the 1775 law left enforcement of ''discipline'' and ''obedience'' in the army to the hetman, Branicki required an oath of allegiance to himself personally rather than to the king or the Republic. Unable to find a flaw in the legality of the oath, Stanislaw August and Stackelberg resolved to change the law at the next diet. They feared that Branicki sought to use the army in support of a *coup d'état*.(23) Branicki's assistant, Colonel Józef Mierzejewski, was then collecting signatures in the provinces on petitions protesting alleged illegalities committed by the Permanent Council. Fearing that Mierzejewski might collect signatures for an anti-government confederation, Stackelberg declared publicly that the three partitioning powers would allow no change in the Polish constitution.(15)

As Branicki asserted his military privileges, Marshal Lubomirski claimed a monopoly over judicial affairs by refusing to sign a paper setting up courts with parliamentary delegates as judges to try political offenses *(sądy sejmowe)*.(16) A dramatic conflict occured over the rights of Jews to do business in and around Warsaw. In July 1775, August Sułkowski used his authority as Marshal of the Permanent Council to sponsor a Jewish settlement called ''New Jerusalem'' on his property inside Warsaw's city limits, though outside her city gates.(17) Christian merchants protested this violation of laws forbidding Jews to live in Warsaw. Since the Marshal's office gave Lubomirski authority over the city he responded by sending guards to knock down the settlement and disperse the inhabitants. Sułkowski complained to Stackelberg that the Council's decrees were being disregarded (although Lubomirski had a better case legally). He also seized on the accidental presence of three Russian soldiers in the Jewish settlement at the time of Lubomirski's raid to fabricate an alleged Opposition plan to attack the Russian army. Stackelberg advised Sułkowski to complain directly to St. Petersburg and he himself used the incident in his arguments to the Russian court for permission to increase the power of the Permanent Council.(18)

Another conflict between the Opposition and the Permanent Council arose over the Justice Department's attempt to require written reports from the provincial Tribunals composed of judges elected by local dietines. Although this simple requirement interfered in no way with the freedom of judges to decide as they pleased, the Opposition portrayed it as a move towards appellate jurisdiction. The use of army detachments to execute court decrees further angered traditionalists even though poor enforcement had long been a problem. Another point of dispute between the Opposition and the Council involved the statute granting the marshal of the Permanent Council the title *wielmożny* (an honorific composed of the words ''great'' and ''powerful''), customarily reserved for senators, as well as precedence over ministers.(19)

Stackelberg sympathized with the Permanent Council's complaints and announced that he would go to Petersburg in early 1776 to win his court's approval for legislation strengthening the Council. Before leaving, the ambassador consulted with Stanisław August. They agreed to return to the traditional even-year pattern by scheduling a diet for the following fall (1776) which would reduce the powers of the ministers, particularly the *hetmen*. Stackelberg expressed confidence that Branicki did not have enough influence at the Russian court to block further reduction of his authority and assured the king that the guarantee given by the partitioning powers would not stand in the way of the proposed changes.(20)

Stanisław August and the Russian ambassador planned to hold the diet as a confederation since confederated diets made decisions by majority vote instead of requiring unanimity as did "free" diets and generally held deputies under tighter discipline. They also decided to organize the confederation as late as possible so as the forestall possible opposition counter-confederations. In the hope of winning support among the lesser nobility, the king and the ambassador chose Andrzej Mokronowski, the popular head of the former French party, to be marshal of the confederated diet. Tomasz Oginski, Lithuanian Grand Secretary and a dependent of the king's, was to become Mokronowski's assistant as Lithuanian Marshal of the Confederation. He actually did most of the work at the 1776 diet since Mokronowski fell ill.(21)

Stanisław August prepared written arguments for Stackelberg to use at the Russian court. In his memorial on "Changes in the Affairs of the King of Poland since 1768", the king argued that a reduction in the hetman's power would be advantageous. What is more, he proved that the power which the hetmen enjoyed in 1775 came from legislation passed at the Russian-dominated diets of 1768 and 1775, and not from Polish traditional practice. Poniatowski drew an analogy between the problems of the army and the rest of Poland to illustrate the need for wholesale constitutional improvement. Like Stackelberg, Stanisław August laid stress on the continued weakness of the Polish government which, he claimed violated the tacit agreement leading to the king's adherence to the Russian party.(22)

Stackelberg arrived in Petersburg in January 1776 to urge the Russian court to give the Permanent Council supremacy over the ministers. He predicted renewed civil strife in Poland if the Permanent Council were not strengthened, with the consequent danger of Prussian and Austrian intervention. In his opinion, Russia need not fear that Poland would become strong enough to become independent because the Permanent Council was only an "administrative service" and not a legislative body.(23)

The Polish Opposition did not let Stackelberg go unchallenged in Petersburg. When Branicki heard of the ambassador's impending mission, he solicited an invitation for himself from Potemkin, but did not arrive in Petersburg until March 1(N.S.) (24) He was accompanied this time by Stanisław Lubomirski's son-in-law, Ignacy Potocki, who brought a comprehensive set of arguments drawn up by the Opposition. Potocki was to inform the Russian court that it had gained the hatred of the bulk of the Polish nobles by putting its trust in "unsure, fickle, (and) self-interested" persons like Poniński and Sułkowski. Russia could regain her popularity in Poland by turning instead to "a friendly party composed of virtuous citizens" who understood that Russian and Polish interests coincided, thus securing stability within Poland and international harmony. The Opposition requested the recall of ambassador Stackelberg since, they said, he was the architect of Russia's misguided policy. Potocki asked to be assured of a free hand at the dietines which were scheduled for the fall.(25)

When Branicki and Potocki reached Petersburg, they met a cold reception. Stackelberg had not only won over the Empress to his plans, he had made the Opposition the subject of enmity in court circles. Potocki found that Stackelberg had used the incident of the Jewish merchants of New Jerusalem so effectively that even "the most neutral persons showed themselves . . . sensitive to the supposed insult to the Russian army."(26) In desperation, Branicki accused Stanisław August of seeking to emulate Gustav III of Sweden who had thrown off Russian influence in 1772 and had become an absolute, independent monarch.(27)

None of Branicki's and Potocki's arguments worked on Panin, who treated Branicki particularly harshly, or on Catherine. The Empress reproved Branicki sharply telling the Hetman in the presence of Antoni Deboli, Stanisław August's envoy to Russia, that "she would not permit him to call himself a friend of Russia except on the condition that he follow . . . the king, his benefactor."(28) Failure reduced the proud Branicki to begging Potemkin for help to insure "that my person is not harmed".(29). Potocki fared no better and was reprimanded by vice-chancellor Ostermann.(30)

Stackelberg left Petersburg on March 24 in complete triumph escorted by Potemkin, Prince Josef Lobkovitz, the Austrian ambassador, and other dignitaries. He reached Warsaw on April 11 with a letter from Catherine to Stanisław August which he could show publicly. The Empress affirmed her friendship for the Polish king and her desire "to maintain the government which she and the (Polish) nation succeeded in establishing", i.e., the Permanent Council.

Catherine expressed concern over opposition to the Council and inisted that the institution be respected. Her assurance that Stackelberg was the "only one I give my orders to and consequently is the sole individual who has the right to speak in my name" enabled Stanisław August to refute Branicki's claim of influence.(31)

Stackelberg also carried instructions, mainly dealing with tactics, which he could show only to the Polish king. The Empress ordered her ambassador to maintain Stanisław August's royal prerogatives and to take the king into "his most intimate confidence" as long as he "continues to follow the same (i.e., pro-Russian) disposition". Catherine instructed Stackelberg to work with Stanisław August "to give the Permanent Council the authority and the power required to make it useful." Either a free or a confederated diet might be employed to this end. Catherine stated a preference for peaceful means of overcoming resistance but authorized Stackelberg to use force, if necessary.(32)

The Opposition had a chance to state its views publicly at the end of February when Stanisław August began the lengthy preparations needed to hold the diet. In line with tradition, the king sent letters to all senators requesting their advice on matters to be discussed at the dietines.(33) Stanisław Lubomirski, Crown Great Marshal and head of the Opposition, replied that the Permanent Council had overstepped its authority and "appropriated to itself the rights that the Republic confided to different government agencies." He feared that such violations could lead to the breakdown of civil authority and "the last degree of anarchy." Lubomirski also complained that taxes were too high and attacked the commission arranging sale of the estates of the disbanded Jesuit order.(34)

Similarly, Seweryn Rzewuski, Crown Field General and Lubomirski's son-in-law, objected to "the Permanent Council, which combines consultative, executive, legislative, and judicial authority, and is incomprehensible to the nation which, when it comes to understand it, will find it unbearable." In line with his military profession, Rzewuski requested curtailment of civilian expenditures and increased investment in the army.(35) Branicki, Crown Great General, also maintained that the Permanent Council had exceeded its legal authority. Recognizing that abolition of the Council was scarcely likely, he asked that it be prevented from committing future "arbitrary acts."(36)

Faced with hostility, Stanisław August turned to his supporters. Antoni Tyzenhauz, Lithuanian Court Treasurer, acted as the king's representative throughout the vast Lithuanian province. Michał Poniatowski, the king's brother and Bishop of Płock, directed efforts in

Mazowsze where the king's favorite nephew and namesake was elected deputy to the diet. Royalist forces in Krakow and Lublin were headed by Ignacy Przebendowski. Stackelberg placed his followers at the king's disposition but Stanisław August found some too much compromised by their reputation for corruption to be of use. He turned to Kazimierz Raczyński, Castellan of Poznań, to direct affairs in Wielkopolska rather than to August Sułkowski for this reason. Bishop Młodziejowski acted as intermediary between the king and the Russian Party.(37)

While Stanisław August dealt with Polish preparations for the dietines, Stackelberg contacted the representatives of Prussia and Austria to seek their support in accordance with instructions from the Russian empress.(38) Baron Karl Reviczky, Austrian ambassador to Poland, had already received instructions from his court to cooperate with the Russian ambassador. Reviczky sought to influence leaders of the Opposition who owned estates in Galicia, under Austria since the first partition, but without much success.(39) Prussia lacked substantial numbers of "mixed subjects" (i.e., Poles with estates in both Poland and Prussia) over whom it could exercise control but Frederick authorized heavy expenditures for political manipulation in Poland. The Prussian king instructed his minister, Gideon Benoit, "to act in perfect accord and concern with Count Stackelberg".(40)

Stackelberg also circulated a proclamation in order "to leave the Polish and Lithuanian nations in no doubt as to the real sentiments of Her Majesty, the Empress of all the Russias." He cautioned the nobles not to believe "false insinuations" spread by the Opposition in the aim of making "suspect the lively and sincere interest that Russia has in the good of the Republic." He warned of the futility of opposition since Russia, Austria, and Prussia stood in complete agreement. He did not, however, go beyond generalities about the legislation that he would support at the diet. More important, circulation of the proclamation provided an excellent pretext for sending armed detachments of Russian troops to every dietine to oppose the contingents raised by the magnates. Stackelberg was refused additional Russian soldiers and more money by Petersburg.(41)

The Opposition resisted pressure from the three partitioning powers. To gain supporters for their cause at the dietines, Branicki toured the Polish Ukraine with cartloads of clothing, shoes, arms, and spirits which he distributed to the local nobility. Adam Czartoryski appealed to traditional patriotism in Wolynia and Podolia by dressing in Polish national costume instead of his usual dress à la française and distributed huge sums as "loans", mostly in Lithuania, to the lesser nobles. Other magnates acted similarly in their home districts. The Opposition also prepared armed strength to act at the dietines. Branicki mobilzed part of the Polish army at places where dietines were to meet and Adam Czartoryski brought the guards regiment which he commanded from Warsaw to Lithuania. Hetman Ogiński unsuccessfully petitioned the Permanent Council for reinforcements for his Lithuanian detachments of the army.(42)

The Opposition encouraged its supporters with vain promises that it, not Stanisław August, was supported by Russia. Branicki had written from Petersburg to friends in Poland that the Russian court had decided to deny Stackelberg funds for political manipulation in Poland (when he had, in fact, received substantial sums) and that Catherine had showed her dissatisfaction with Stackelberg by failing to give him any presents. The hetman returned to Poland with further embellishments. He said that Stackelberg had instructions to maintain the Permanent Council ''in its legal bounds'', hence not to extend its authority. Branicki reported further that Russia would sent no more troops into Poland, that the Russian army already present would not interfere with the dietines, and that Russia desired a free diet. All these claims were false, designed to raise the morale of the Opposition and prepare them for activity at the dietines. The Opposition countered Stackelberg's declaration with public letters accusing the Permanent Council of despotism, calling for an increase in the hetmen's power, complaining about high taxes, and calling for an augmentation of the size of the army.(43)

Where both Russia and Opposition forces met, dietines were characterized by violent clashes. The bloodiest struggle occurred in Ciechanów where a noble named Zieliński led an attack on the Russian troops killing their captain. Thirty Poles died in the struggle and Zieliński, mortally wounded, confessed that Branicki had induced him to attack.(44) Additional skirmishes at Łomża and Słonim permitted Stackelberg to report to his court, with considerable exaggeration, that the Opposition had intended a ''Sicilian Vespers''.(45) Hetman Ogiński resided in Słonim, but Branicki's nephew, Prince Kazimierz Nestor Sapieha sneaked in during the night. He surrendered to the Russians permit him to enter the church where the dietine was to be held so Saphieha sneaked in during the night. He surrendered to the Russians the next day to prevent bloodshed but his example inspired his followers to elect him deputy to the diet anyway. The Russian commander at Wilno handled a similar situation more efficiently. He place his troops at the entrance to the dietine and excluded members of the Opposition.(46)

Stanisław August's lieutenants used the technique of ''doubling'' dietines in a number of locations to assure their supremacy. When the royalists failed to suppress the Opposition, they adjourned to a different place to hold their own elections and debates. Deputies thus chosen went to Warsaw later for the meeting of the full diet and sought accreditation. Doubled dietines occurred in Lublin, Słonim, Łęczyca, and Ciechanów.(47)

In addition to electing deputies to the diet, the local dietines also wrote instructions for them. The binding nature of these instructions had been abolished in 1764, but they still reflected the political opinions which predominated at the dietines. Opposition-controlled dietines demanded that no confederation or delegation be organized at the diet, that the Permanent Council be held strictly to the 1775 laws or be abolished altogether, that foreign armies (i.e. Russian troops) evacuate Poland, and that any citizen summoning foreign armies into Poland be severely punished. Some dietines specifically recommended that power over the army be fully restored to the Hetmen. Dietines controlled by the king's supporters through the help of Russian troops restricted their requests to routine matters, although Kiev asked that the military and treasury commission be abolished and Luck requested "clarifications" of the laws of the 1775 diet.(48)

With the dietines concluded, the king and the Russian ambassador made final preparations for the diet. On July 17, Stanislaw August showed Stackelberg a list of deputies chosen by the dietines and their instructions. The king asked formally for permission to organize a confederation. By organizing a confederation, the diet would suspend the *liberum veto* so that decisions would be made by majority vote. Thus, the small number of Opposition deputies who would succeed in entering the diet would not cast their *nie pozwalam*. Stackelberg and Stanisław August decided to summon their supporters to Warsaw a week before the scheduled opening of the diet and, in accordance with August Sulkowski's suggestion, determined to organize the confederation in the Permanent Council. The confederation would be open for all to join, although the king's supporters would form a majority. In fact the confederation was to force the hetmen to join so that they would be bound by the confederation's decisions. Only members of the confederation would be permitted to sit in the diet.(49)

The king's party kept this plan secret extraordinarily well but the formation of a confederation was such an obvious and expected tactic that some Opposition leaders came to Warsaw in August to make their own preparations. Branicki, Czartoryski, and Rzewuski sought reconciliation with the king but only on the condition that no confederation be organized. Several days later, Branicki and Rzewuski joined with the ministers to present a memorial to the king declaring that he had no right to organize a confederated diet since the dietines had been called for a free diet. Six of the sixteen ministers signed the protest and two more were favorable.(50)

The Opposition also took its campaign to the public through the distribution of pamphlets. An anonymous "Letter by the King's Chamberlain about Warsaw before the Diet" was a satire playing on national pride by attacking Stanisław August's foreign advisors. After examining the Polish governmental system, the author came to the familiar conclusion that the Permanent Council intended to establish despotism but that the independent ministers, who loved the old laws, could save Poland. Another "Letter by a Certain Senator to a Citizen" accused the Permanent Council of exceeding its legal powers by invading areas of administration served by the ministers and governing commissions. Another pamphlet was devoted to proving the impropriety and illegality of any confederation that the king might try to organize.(51) The royalists did not reply, no doubt feeling secure in their political supremacy.

Without responding to the Opposition's protest, Stanisław August initiated the formalities necessary to establish a confederation. On September 23, Bishop Tomasz Ostrowski took the floor in the Permanent Council, which met in the Royal Palace, to make a speech warning of new dangers to Polish territorial integrity which might arise if the forthcoming diet were disorderly. In order to prevent disputes about the credentials of rival delegations from doubled dietines, Ostrowski asked that Poland present a united front by means of a confederation. The members of the Council then signed a previously prepared act of confederation which the king presented. Stanisław August also signed. Approximately one hundred senators and deputies who had been enjoying a banquet at the palace of Michał Poniatowski came to the Royal Palace to place their signatures on the act. The confederation elected the nominees of Stanisław August and Stackelberg, Mokronowki and Ogiński, as its marshals. After notifying foreign diplomats that the confederation now exercized supreme power in Poland, the marshals of the confederation sent representatives to administrative bodies requiring their members to join. Branicki signed only when threatened with suspension from office. Russian troops entered Warsaw while the royalists formed their confederation. The Russians set up camp on the square in front of the Royal Palace where the diet met as well as elsewhere in the city.(52)

The confederated diet opened on August 26 with royal guards placed at the doors of the legislative chamber to prevent persons who had not adhered to the confederation from entering. About thirty Opposition deputies from the doubled dietines were thus excluded, even though some like Ignacy Potocki and Kazimierz Sapieha, young firebrands of the Opposition, had asked to be permitted to join the confederation. Protests during the diet to the effect that ''numerous deputies of the Crown and Lithuanian provinces stand unheard at the doors of the legislative temple'' went unheeded. The confederation failed to wrest control of the entrance to the Senate chamber from Marshal Lubomirski's guards.(53)

With most opponents excluded and the rest neutralized by the royalist majority, the diet instructed Chancellor Młodziejowski to petition ambassador Stackelberg for permission ''to improve the internal governmental apparatus.'' Stackelberg replied affirmatively, of course, adding only that the Russian empress expected Poles to make no changes without discussing them first with him.(54)

After several days of formalities, Lithuanian Marshal Ogiński introduced a bill entitled ''Explanation of the Power of the Permanent Council'' designed to restore internal order to Poland and insure enforcement of the laws.(55) The small group of Oppositionists remaining objected vociferously to strengthening the Permanent Council. Marshal Lubomirski saw in the bill ''the road to slavery, anarchy, and the ruination of citizens''. He predicted that by means of future ''explanations'' the king would destroy the Republic and transform it into a despotism.(56) Hetman Rzewuski believed that this dangerous moment was already at hand. ''We are standing over precipice'', he announced grandiloquently, ''and one more step will finish us.''(57) When the matter came to a vote later that day, however, the Opposition could mobilize only 32 votes in the lower house against 150 royalist supporters. The upper chamber vote came slightly closer: 12 to 42. A revised bill (with several textual but no substantive changes) submitted several days later became, once again, the subject of heated attacks by Lubomirski and others. Lubomirski denounced it as contrary to the Fundamental Laws of 1768 which, he reminded the diet, threatened to punish any one proposing constitutional changes. Procedural squabbles and an attempted filibuster delayed matters but the final vote passed the bill by a margin of 49 to 12 in the Senate and 110 to 16 in the Chamber of Deputies.(58)

According to the final text, an ''Explanation of the Establishment of the Permanent Council'' had become necessary because of insufficient respect paid to the Council in its first year of existence. To avoid disputes arising from the "ambiguity of law" creating overlapping executive authorities through ministers, commissions and departments, the Council gained the right to "interpret" laws and enforce execution of its decrees by suspending from office any minister or other governmental official who continued to disobey the council's decision. The Council did not become absolute, however, because the diet could review its actions and overturn decisions.(59) At succeeding diets in our period (1778, 1780, 1782, 1784, and 1786), each diet formed a Committee for the Examination of the Permanent Council *(Komisya do examinwania Rady Nieustającey)* which read the records of the preceding cadence of the Council. In each year, the diet overruled several inconsequential decisions.(60) In 1782, the Opposition made a concerted but unsuccessful attempt to censure Council involvement in the arrest of Bishop Kajetan Sołtyk of Krakow.

A separate law formulated more precisely the "obligations and authority of departments in the Permanent Council" in order to solve specific problems which had arisen in 1775-1776. Most important, the Military Department absorbed the functions of the Crown and Lithuanian Military Commissions. All four hetmen gained the right to sit in the Department, but they could be outvoted by elected members. While in 1775 the hetmen had enjoyed complete command over the army, the 1776 law barred them from giving orders to any troops without authorization from the Military Department. They were specifically prohibited from requiring an oath of allegiance to themselves, as Branicki had done. The king regained control over four guards regiments which the 1775 diet had taken from him as well as the right to promote officers, which he had lost at the same time.(61)

While reducing the power of the ministers, the diet also administered a rebuke to those who had profited through corruption of the partition diet. Many pensions and gratifications were cancelled and an investigation committee established to prevent further corrupt alienation of Jesuit estates. Unfortunately, the diet could not recover those estates already lost.(62)

An encouraging sign for future reform was the law authorizing compilation of a law code to replace the voluminous and frequently contradictory mass of legislative precedent by which cases were judged. Stanisław August proposed Andrzej Zamoyski as head of the committee charged with this task. His name proved so popular, due to his patriotic resignation as chancellor in 1768 rather than sign an obnoxious decree, that the diet accepted the measure by acclamation without the customary three-day wait.(63) The deputies would have done better to have listened carefully. The bill instructed Zamoyski not to "tie himself to any piece of old legislation'', but to work in such a way that ''natural justice be the prime factor''. The deputies were too excited by the prospect of correcting ''abuses resulting from the number, backwardness, contradiction, and various inaccuracies of laws'' to consider the consequences of so broad a mandate.(64)

The 1776 diet enacted a number of minor acts of interest. Poland became the second state in Europe (after Prussia) to abolish torture in criminal proceedings. The death penalty for witchcraft was abolished. Sumptuary laws (affecting the lower orders only) were passed with the stated purpose of improving Poland's unfavorable balance of payments. Other measures included a vote of appreciation for the Załuski brothers for starting a public library and a guarantee of a foreign loan for Stanisław August.(65)

Only prolongation of the diet twice permitted it to transact as much business as it did. Organization of a confederation had prevented the ''explosion'' of the diet by a *liberum veto* and allowed the majority to enact legislation sealing the supremacy of the king and the Permanent Council in Poland. But debates continued interminably and little legislation of value was enacted. The king hoped for further reform. But in succeeding years, as in 1776, he had to seek Russia's permission since she, as well as the other partitioning powers, had reaffirmed their guarantee the preservation of traditional Polish liberties.(66)

CHAPTER III

THE LIMITS OF REFORM

King Stanisław August recognized and appreciated the gains made through legislation enacted by the recent confederated diet but he ardently desired additional reforms. As he explained to a correspondent, "the diet has taken . . . several important steps toward the improvement of the government of this country. However, what remains to be done is much greater than what has been done."(1) The king preferred to take needed measures with Russia's assistance, but he was prepared to act independently, if necessary.

In order to convince the Russian court of the need for reform, Stanisław August dispatched his young nephew and namesake, Stanisław Poniatowski, to St. Petersburg. Prince Stanisław, who had been a deputy at the 1776 diet, ostensibly was charged with conveying the king's thanks to Catherine II for the legislation of 1776. In private, however, the king told him to enter into far-ranging political discussions. The prince's written instructions directed him to seek a confederated diet in 1778 which would enact more changes in the structure of the Permanent Council and new taxes. The prince could be more specific in free discussion at the court.(2)

Prince Stanisław Poniatowski left Warsaw at the beginning of December 1776 and arrived in Petersburg two and a half weeks later.(3) Catherine received him extremely well and presented him with the order of St. Andrew. This personal success seemed so significant that Alexis Husarzewski, the Polish king's well-informed agent in Gdańsk, recommended leaving Prince Stanislaw in Petersburg as a permanent ambassador-extraordinary, while the Marshal of the 1776 Diet, Andrzej Mokronowski, speculated that Prince Stanisław might seek permission to succeed his uncle on the Polish throne.(4) Nevertheless, Prince Stanisław failed to translate his personal success into political gain. Learning that his nephew could not draw Russian leaders into serious discussion, the Polish king recalled him to Warsaw expressing satisfaction, however, with the impression made on Russian society. Despite the failure in Petersburg, the king continued in the months ahead to think of a confederated diet which would enact significant reform.(5)

The king also tried to initiate a *rapprochement* with the Opposition in order to lessen his dependence on the Russian ambassador. Stanisław August met Hetman Branicki several times in the spring and summer of 1777 to plan a marriage between Branicki's nephew, Kazimierz Nestor Sapieha, and the king's niece and the two appeared to be on very good terms once again.(6) During that summer, Stanisław August travelled to the provinces to meet with Opposition leaders. He went first to Puławy for eight days to see his uncle and long-time political opponent, August Czartoryski, who received him with impressive ceremony. The king then proceeded to Wołczyń to visit August's son, Prince Adam Czartoryski, "who received him with truer cordiality than his father (had)."(7) Personal diplomacy failed, however, to overcome the differences between the king and his opponents. Even the projected marriage fell through.

In addition to maneuvering at home and in Russia for political advantage, Stanisław August looked to the outside world to achieve at least the appearance of independence of the partitioning powers and, if the opportunity arose, perhaps even the reality. He hoped to reestablish diplomatic relations with Turkey, which had refused to recognize his coronation because of the use of Russian troops and France, which had supported his enemies of the Bar Confederation. Great Britain, which had opposed the first partition, showed little interest in Polish affairs after that partition gave Frederick of Prussia control over the Vistula.(8)

Stanisław August received permission from ambassador Stackelberg, who consulted Russian ambassador Alexius Stakiev in Turkey, to send an envoy to Istanbul to negotiate a trade agreement. The king made the happy choice of a Swiss named Charles Boscamp, who had been naturalized as a Polish citizen under the name Lasopolski. Not only did Boscamp speak fluent Turkish, but he had a history of good relations with the Russians. Despite fears that the Turks might reject the Polish envoy as a Russian spy, Boscamp was well received by the Grand Vizir and the Sultan. The Turks further showed good will by dispatching Numan Bey as envoy to Poland in order to convey Turkey's belated recognition of Stanisław August Poniatowski as King of Poland.(9)

The unexpected ease with which Poland gained Russian and Turkish agreement to her entrance into mid-East diplomacy owed itself to new tensions which had arisen between the two countries. In the spring of 1777, the Russian candidate for Crimean Khan, Sahin-Girey, triumphed over his Ottoman-backed rival thanks to Russian armed intervention. A serious revolt in October 1777, which the rebels portrayed as a defense of Islam against the Christians, brought Turkey and Russia to the brink of war. In these circumstances, Russia hoped that Boscamp would act as a friendly mediator while the Porte wanted to find out whether Poland was ready to throw off the Russian yoke.(10) Stackelberg had Stanisław August have his representative "maintain the appearance of neutrality "in order to give moreweight to pro-Russian sentiments expressed in discussions with the Turks.(11)

Numan Bey reached Warsaw in July 1777. Despite squabbles over ceremonial propriety, Warsaw received him enthusiastically. The Polish king and many of his subjects took pleasure in social relations with the Turk, who proved flexible enough to drink wine and kind enough to allow Poles to try their schoolbook knowledge of Turkish on him. Yet the Polish treasury had to pay dearly for the privilege of Numan Bey's company — fifty ducats daily, 106,896 zlp. in all — and day by day his company became less desirable. Stackelberg found the Turkish envoy's presence worrisome although the Turk rarely discussed politics and generally restricted his activities to social gatherings. The Russian ambassador feared possible political cabals between Numan Bey and the royalists as well as Numan Bey and the Opposition.(12)

The Russian ambassador need not have worried. Numan Bey saw Poland's political and military dependence on Russia very clearly. He sensed that Poland would not and could not offer Turkey any help in her struggle against Russia. On the contrary, Turkey began to worry lest further relations with Poland created a climate in which the governors of the frontier provinces might engage in independent action in concert with the Polish Opposition and bring Turkey once more into war against Russia. Numan Bey left Warsaw for Turkey in April 1778.(13)

Numan Bey's passivity troubled the Russians, but Boscamp-Laspolski's active course in Istanbul alarmed them seriously. After arranging for Numan Bey's mission to Poland, Boscamp tried to negotiate a trade agreement and sought to establish a permanent Polish mission in Turkey. To accomplish all these projects, Boscamp turned to the French ambassador, Georges Le Bas, for help, showing him letters from Warsaw which stated that the French court had assured Stanislaw August that it would assist him with the Porte. Le Bas, however, had received no such instructions from Versailles and declined to act.(14)

Stanisław August hoped to gain French assistance by dispatching his trusted Swiss advisor, Maurice Glaire, to France at the same time he sent Boscamp to Turkey. The king had high hopes for the mission since France thought it worthwhile maintaining three non-accredited representatives to inform the French court of Polish developments and had already in 1776 shown itself interested in relations with Poland.

Stackelberg had given his approval of secret correspondence between Andrzej Mokronowski and the French court before the 1776 diet in order to win over members of the former French Party.(15)

Meanwhile, private parties in France expressed their interest in relations with Poland. The count d'Artois, brother of the king of France, proposed to Stanisław August that he resign his throne in favor of the count and move to Lorraine as Stanisław Leszczyński had so many years ago.(16) Stanisław August never took this offer seriously but a second proposal came through the French ambassador in Vienna who told an old friend, Marshal Franciszek Rzewuski, that a match could be arranged between Stanisław August and the daughter of the Prince Condé which would assure the king 50,000 ducats annually. Princess Lubomirska entered the marital sweepstakes by proposing, on her own authority, that Stanisław August marry archduchess Elizabeth of Austria. Rumors spread both before and after the 1776 diet that the Polish king was about to contract an important marriage alliance.(17)

On arrival in France, Maurice Glaire arranged an interview with the French foreign minister, count Charles de Vergennes, in which he sought to convince Vergennes to establish formal diplomatic relations with Poland. Responding in diplomatic phrases, Vergennes stressed that "Russia is the power which seems most interested in guarding Poland's existence and even in improving her form of government." More directly, Vergennes warned Glaire that France would do nothing to oppose Russia. In fact, France desired "to sever all the knots of intrigue which have held France and Poland together for so long."(18)

The verdict, then, was that France would send no envoy to Poland for fear that "on the sight of a French minister entering Warsaw, the Polish imagination would immediately catch fire" and that "restless elements" would take advantage of the occasion to act against Russia. Having made it clear that Stanisław August could expect no help, Vergennes expressed his sympathy for Poland's plight. He acknowledged that the 1776 diet did "nothing in comparison with what has to be done" and led the Polish envoy to the conclusion that Vergennes "would like a revolution in Poland like the one he successfully directed in Sweden.(19) Before Glaire could meet with Vergennes a second time he received a hurried message from the Polish king to leave France immediately.(20)

Polish diplomatic activities in Istanbul and Paris had offended Russia. Stakiev complained from the Ottoman capital that Boscamp gave support to the Turkish war faction and led them to expect Polish aid in case of war with Russia. Panin therefore instructed Stackelberg to procure Poland's withdrawal from the design of arranging a permanent mission to Turkey.(21) Boscamp did not have to leave Turkey but remained under deep suspicion and the Russian ambassador had him followed for the remainder of his stay. On one bizarre occasion, Stakiev himself tailed the Polish envoy to a state dinner in the inappropriate disguise of a lower-class Englishman.(22)

The Glaire mission fared still worse. The Russian ambassador in France, Prince Ivan Bariatinsky, complained to Stackelberg about Glaire's conduct. Stackelberg then wrote Stanisław August a harsh note denouncing the king's ''machiavel-ism'' for giving Glaire ostensibly a non-political mission while really sending him to negotiate a political alliance. Stackelberg followed up his note with an interview during which he threatened the Polish king with loss of political support. Stanisław August hurriedly instructed Glaire to leave France; he told him to travel back slowly through Italy in the vain hope that Stackelberg would change his mind.(23)

Stanisław August's foreign policy manoeuvres of 1777 brought no result but they had been realistically conceived. Powerful individuals at the French court like the Prince Condé and the count d'Artois, intrigued with him. Furthermore, the French foreign ministry prepared a memorial on Poland which concluded that alliance with Poland would be in France's interest. The author, M. Deflotte, believed that Poland would increase in strength under Stanisław August's leadership and regain something of her former position in the European state system. Russia would permit France to gain influence in Poland in order to gain French assistance against Austrian and Prussian intrigues in Poland. The author suggested that France's dignity would not permit her to become the suitor of such a weak country as Poland but she should show her friendship and wait until Poland sought her out. France should then recommend that Poland sent an unpublicized mission to negotiate. These suggestions so closely resemble the actual events that it may be concluded that France led Stanisław August into his diplomatic fiasco.(24)

Stanisław August met further disappointment in his sponsorship of the law code which Andrzej Zamoyski had drawn up in accordance with the authorization of the 1776 diet. Zamoyski gathered a distinguished group of co-workers: Joachim Chreptowicz (Lithuanian vice-chancellor); Bishop Krzysztof Szembek, Michał Węgrzecki, a lawyer; Antoni Rogalski, head of Zamoyski's personal archive; and Józef Wybicki, author of the *Patriotic Letters*. Felix Łojko, historian and economist, and Hugo Kołłątaj, reformer of the Jagiellonian University, also contributed while not regular members of the committee. The committee based its work on Polish legal precedents but also consulted philosophical and legal works from abroad.(25)

The Zamoyski Law Code offered Poland a number of progressive steps, some of which were camouflaged by citations from old legislation. The most important single provision of the proposed law code followed a 1492 law granting the second, fourth, and succeeding sons of peasants the right to leave the land on which their father was enserfed. They could either go to the cities and find work or remain on the land as free peasants with the right to appeal to royal courts in case of legal disputes with the local landlord. Furthermore, nobles were threatened with strong penalties for injuring peasants physically; a serf would gain freedom if attacked. Another section required that each parish maintain a school for peasants between St. Martin's Day (in November) and Easter.(26)

Cities also received some advantages from the Zamoyski Code. Civic authorities received protection against nobles living within their gates. The cities could force nobles to pay taxes, obey municipal court decisions, and could regulate manufactures under noble ownership. Cities also gained the right to purchase land within three miles of their boundaries and the right to hold national congresses to discuss inter-urban problems. Other provisions of the Law Code encouraged the establishment of joint stock companies in which burghers and nobles could join. Finally, the large cities gained permission to send representatives to the diet to present requests. Harsh restrictions in imitation of German policy were put on Jews who could not live in cities without specific permission.(27)

A final area of innovation was church-state relations where Poland was to imitate Austria and France by requiring state permission to publish papal bulls. Church courts were stripped of appeal to Rome. A Clerical Tribunal was set up as the highest clerical court. Other anti-clerical proposals limited the freedom of nobles to transfer landed estates to the Church, fixed the lowest age of entry into religious orders at twenty-four for men and twenty for women. Piarists, Theatines, and several other "useful" bodies received exemptions. Clerical courts were restricted in their right to judge financial cases relating to estates and tithes. (28) One directly political measure proposed stripping landless nobles of their patents of nobility.(29)

The provisions of the Law Code offended several powerful vested interests. The Church resented the restrictions placed on it, the nobility feared any change in the status of the peasant, and the Russian ambassador felt that Stanisław August had improperly set out on a course of political reform through the medium of the law code. The Jews, naturally, had no opportunity to defend themselves, but the Church and the nobles entered into a spirited polemical war with the Law Code.

Political opposition to the law code appeared after its publication in late 1777. The Papal nuncio, Giovanni Archetti, was disabused of his illusion that Bishop Szembek and king Stanisław August would prevent the committee from proposing "anti-clerical" ideas. A private appeal to the king and the bishops failed.(30) Archetti appealed to the dietines to oppose the code. Several responded with protests that the committee had gone beyond what the diet had authorized it to do and that the Code contained "more political changes than legal explanations."(31) The Ministerial Party made part of its platform that "the law code be set aside for deliberation."(32) Stackelberg also joined forces with the Nuncio, objecting to provisions in the Code which would have given the king limited powers of pardon. The ambassador considered this a change of substantial magnitude which should have been discussed first with Russia. As a result, he went to Archetti and offered his services. Lithuanian nobles also opposed the Code on the grounds that it replaced Lithuania's autonomous legal statute; but in fact, the Zamoyski Code incorportated the Lithuanian statute without change.(33) Under pressure from the Papal Nuncio, the Russian ambassador, and much of the nobility, Stanislaw August agreed to withhold the Code until 1780, supposedly so that the Polish nation could deliberate its provisions at leisure. He let it be known abroad that the Code "did not find that degree of finish and maturity that such a work should possess."(34)

The situation had not improved by 1780, however. Anti-Zamoyski forces triumphed at the dietines in Poznań, Lublin, Wilno, Grodno, Smoleńsk, Mińsk, Wolyń and Podole. Even at the dietine at Środy in Royal Prussia, where Protestant nobles could normally be counted on to support the king's wishes, Józef Wybicki felt such resentment directed against him for his part in drawing up the Code that he fled before the start of the dietine.(35) Hoping to save the Code from defeat, the king proposed another two-year delay. Stackelberg and Stanisław Lubomirski agreed, but the hot spirits of the lesser nobility prevailed.(36)

During the 1780 diet, a bill to reject the Code was introduced from the floor and deputies began to shout that they would permit no further business until that bill was passed and signed. A slightly amended version introduced the following day, proved too conciliatory in tone for the deputies. The diet finally passed a law stating that "we reject this collection of laws . . . forever and desire that it never be brought up at any future diet."(37) Only the king's nephew, Prince Stanisław Poniatowki, courageously opposed the prevailing sentiment and he dared ask only that the rejection be accomplished "in the gentlest manner."(38)

The near-unanimous hostility of the Lithuanian deputies to the Zamoyski Code underscored the political transformation of the province, a process which acted to Stanisław August's great disadvantage. From 1776 to 1780, Lithuania was ruled by Antoni Tyzenhauz, Lithuanian Court Treasurer, Stanisław August's chief political agent. Combining his ministerial office, which gave him control over the Lithuanian Treasury Commission, and his position as manager of the royal estates in Lithuania, Tyzenhauz enjoyed unrivalled economic power which he used to build a strong political party. In 1775 and 1776, Stackelberg had looked upon Tyzenhauz's activities with favor. He permitted the king to raise the office of Court Treasurer to ministerial rank (giving its occupant a seat in the senate) and encouraged him to channel patronage through Tyzenhauz. Even more important, the Russian ambassador protected Tyzenhauz against charges by the Russian army commander in Lithuania that Tyzenhauz was preparing an anti-Russian insurrection.(39)

Tyzenhauz soon lost the ambassador's favor and paved the way for his own downfall. Stackelberg considered that Tyzenhauz was becoming too independent in his management of the Lithuanian dietines in 1776.(40) In 1777 he showed his displeasure by refusing to intervene in Tyzenhauz's favor when Borchowa, the wife of Polish vice-chancellor Jan Borch, appealed to the Russian empress to help her win a complicated law suit against the Lithuanian Treasurer, who, she alleged, had illegally kidnapped her sister's child in order to enrich himself with the child's patrimony. Borchowa appealed to Petersburg since her estates had passed into the Russian empire by the first partition. Tyzenhauz defended himself by sending a representative to Petersburg to argue that the girl in question was in fact his niece and that he had given her full control of her patrimony when she came of age. Catherine responded positively to Borchowa, however, and sent an official note to Stackelberg directing him to arrange the evocation of the law case from Grodno, where Tyzenhauz controlled the law courts, to Warsaw, where the ambassador could direct the proceedings. The utter unconstitutionality of the Russian proposal (Warsaw having no higher court with powers of evocation) enabled Stanisław August to refuse. Thus, the Borch-Tyzenhauz law suit was tried in Grodno with the expected result — complete victory for the Treasurer.(41)

Despite Stackelberg's failure on this occasion, lines of battle were joined for the future. By encouraging the Treasurer's enemies to intrigue against him, the Russian ambassador hoped to place Stanisław August in closer dependence on him. Stackelberg warned the king several times that civil war might break out in Lithuania between Tyzenhauz and his enemies and reproached the king for failing to heed the desires of the Russian court.(42) The king's family began to urge him to abandon Tyzenhauz and Crown Court Marshal Franciszek Rzewuski offered Stanislaw August substantially more money than Tyzenhauz was paying for managing the royal estates in Lithuania. The king refused so as to retain Tyzenhauz's political services.(43) Michał Zaleski, who had lost part of his estate to Tyzenhauz, and Bishop Kossakowski, related to Borchowa by marriage, campaigned actively among Lithuanian nobles. Hetman Branicki and Prince Adam Czartoryski led a group protesting Tyzenhauz's exercise of power.(44)

Stackelberg and the king's family united in opposing Tyzenhauz. During the 1778 diet, Stackelberg insisted on having the king's nephew by marriage, Ludwik Tyszkiewicz, selected as marshal of the diet in preference to the king's own choice, Tyzenhauz's chief lieutenant, Kazimierz Wolmar.(45) In 1779, Tyszkiewicz renewed his campaign for Lithuanian leadership by seeking to become Marshal of the Lithuanian Tribunal. Stanisław August tried to steer a middle position by unsuccessfully seeking a reconciliation of the two opponents. Finally, he permitted Tyzenhauz to maintain control of the dietines as usual although he urged the Lithuanian to allow his opponents some local victories.(46)

Tyzenhauz did not submit easily to the dimunition of his influence. The efforts of Adam Czartoryski, Michał Ogiński, Joachim Chreptowicz, Michał Zaleski, and Michał Brzostowski went for nothing as Tyzenhauz doubled and even trebled dietines in order to control them. When the Tribunal opened, he successfully challenged the credentials of his opponents from the multiple dietines. Thus, Tyzenhauz succeeded in producing the election of judges favorable to himself although he permitted the election of Tyszkiewicz as marshal in deference to the king and the Russian ambassador.(47)

The one action which the King of Poland could not accept from Tyzenhauz was financial irregularity and here Antoni Tyzenhauz failed. Tyzenhauz had signed a special contract in 1777, making him manager of the royal Lithuanian estates in exchange for monthly payments used to pay off a foreign loan which the king negotiated in 1776.(48) The Court Treasurer met his obligations without difficulty during the first few years but missed the January 1780 payment because his manufactures were draining his capital Stanisław August turned to

Marshal Franciszek Rzewuski for the missing 17,00 ducats.(49) The February installment reached Warsaw almost two weeks late and Stanisław August warned Tyzenhauz that he would abandon him to his enemies if Tyzenhaus could not meet his obligations.(50) When the March payment was also delayed, Stanisław August urged Tyzenhauz to declare bankruptcy but yielded to requests for one more chance.(51) Failure to pay in June sealed Tyzenhauz's fate. Stanisław August refused to help the Treasurer again and sent an agent, Jan Kicki, to Grodno to take possession of the estates.(52)

Even at this point, Stanisław August desired to retain the services of his lieutenant, but pressure from Stackelberg, who got assistance from the Prussian resident, Gideon Blanchot, prevented this. The Russian ambassador threatened to claim the royal estates for Russia since Catherine, as guarantor of the king's foreign loan, could be held legally responsible for the failure to pay.(53) Blanchot charged that Tyzenhauz had abducted artisans from East Prussia to work on his estates.(54) Tyzenhauz returned to Warsaw to fight his dismissal but Stanisław August refused to see him until he resigned his contract for the royal estates in writing. Stackelberg met Tyzenhauz in the king's antechamber and told him that he had been dismissed because his control of Lithuania had caused too many complaints in Petersburg.(55)

Tyzenhauz continued to fight to maintain his position. When he heard that Stanisław August had signed a new contract for the estates with Court Marshal Rzewuski who sent agents to manage them, Tyzenhauz raced back to Grodno. He rapidly transferred all papers, furniture, cattle, and other moveables to his hereditary estates before Rzewuski's men arrived to take possession. Rzewuski's agent, Wincenty Sobolewski, however, gathered some of Tyzenhauz's foes, retook the archive, and expelled Tyzenhauz from his palace by armed force.(56) Nevertheless, Tyzenhauz maintained his control over the dietines for the 1780 Tribunal to save his position by judicial decree. He cited the king, Rzewuski, and Sobolewski for violent assault *(najazd)* and also claimed that the contract granting him control of the royal estates was still in force. The elected judges of the Tribunal, however followed the lead of Bishop Kossakowski, who was supported by armed men under the direction of his brother. As a result, the Tribunal found against Tyzenhauz.(57) Tyzenhauz still maintained partial control over the dietines which elected representatives for the 1780 diet. He lost, however, in Słonim, where Hetman Ogiński gained the upper hand, and in his home city of Grodno, where Bishop Kossakowski remained in control.(58)

The *dénouement* came at the diet which was controlled by Tyzenhauz's enemies. Michał Zaleski, new head of the Lithuanian Treasury Commission, gained authorization for a review of Tyzenhauz's accounts.(59) The Zaleski Commission found great irregularities, charged Tyzenhauz with embezzlement; and demanded that he pay triple damages amounting to 2,627,790.51 zlotys (145,922 ducats). To raise these large sums, the Commission sequestered Tyzenhauz's personal estates. Action before the Lithuanian Tribunal in succeeding years provided final legal sanction for removing Tyzenhauz from management of the royal estates.(60) Financially and politically ruined, the Lithuanian Treasurer declined into acute melancholia and physical collapse. At the urging of the king, the 1784 diet relented and reduced his punishment to simple reimbursement. Since more than that had already been collected, the diet ordered the excess returned.(61) Tyzenhauz died the following year.

While Stanisław August went from defeat to defeat in his efforts to strengthen his position, the Opposition prospered under Austrian patronage. Austria had left Russia with a free hand in Poland in 1776 but the outbreak of the War of the Bavarian Succession convinced her of the need for independent strength. In January 1778, Joseph II of Austria reasserted dynastic claims to the recently vacated Bavarian throne by sending troops into the province. Frederick II of Prussia encouraged minor German princes by promises of military assistance to protest the Austrian action.(62) Poland became involved when Frederick II asked permission to march troops across Polish territory to reach Silesia, the staging area for an attack on Austrian Bohemia.(63) Severely embarrassed and wishing to offend neither Prussia by refusing nor Austria by accepting, Stanisław August and the Permanent Council followed Stackelberg's advice by replying that only the diet could make such decisions.(64) Prussia, taking the reply as tacit permission, moved troops through in good order in April and launched an attack on Bohemia in July.(65)

Austria regarded Polish passivity as friendship towards Prussia. She began a propaganda campaign aimed at developing Polish hostility to Frederick and winning sympathizers to the Austrian cause.(66) Austria had little difficulty here since Prussia had exploited her territorial gains from the first partition to strangle Polish trade along with Vistula. She had also tried on numerous occasions to extend her control beyond the demarcation line set by the 1776 treaty with Poland.(67) Austrian propaganda held out to Poland the prospect of regaining territories lost to Prussia in the first partition.(68)

Prussia formulated ambitious projects to turn Poland against Austria but would take no steps without Russian approval. Frederick believed that a Polish rising against the small Austrian garrison occupying Galicia could be easily organized, or, alternatively, he, thought of organizing a confederation in Poland, but neither Stackelberg nor officials in St. Petersburg agreed.(69) Frederick had to accept a passive role. He was prepared to prevent any hostile move against him, however, by bribing a deputy to cast a *liberum veto* at the 1778 diet, if necessary.(70)

Stackelberg aimed at keeping Poland tranquil during the European crisis by making some concessions to Austria. Just before the start of the 1778 diet, the Russian ambassador sought out his Austrian colleague, Baron Reviczky, to assure him that Russia did not intend to use the diet to pass any anti-Austrian measures despite Russia's alliance with Prussia. As an indication of Russia's good faith, Stackelberg invited members of the Opposition Party to enter the Permanent Council. Prince Adam Czartoryski and Marshal Stanisław Lubomirski, who had vast Galician estates, as well as their political allies, Hetman Franciszek Branicki, Ignacy Potocki, Kazimierz Nestor Sapieha, Józef Mierzejewski, and Kajetan Kurdwanowski would now be in a position to protect Austria's interests.(71)

Austria's Polish friends asserted their independence of the Polish king from the beginning of the Permanent Council session in November 1778. The most colorful incident, as usual, involved Hetman Branicki. In his new role as president of the Military Department, Branicki sought to prevent the king's personal adjutant, General Jan Komarzewski, who had previously attended meetings of the Military Department as the king's representative, from attending meetings unless he remained standing and wore full regulation uniform. The king summoned Branicki to the Royal Palace to tell him that he had excused Komarzewski from obeying Branicki's command but the hetman, standing on his independent rights, swore that he would arrest Komarzewski for insubordination if he failed to obey. The king finally won out but not before Branicki created a scandal with the false claim that Stanisław August had threatened him physically.(72)

Opposition members of the Department of Foreign Affairs insisted on their right to see all correspondence from Polish envoys abroad which had previously been delivered directly to the king. In order to maintain his control over foreign policy, Stanislaw August required the Polish envoys to write two different sets of dispatches, one for the Permanent Council and one for him.(73). Work in the Council slowed down to a halt as the Opposition indulged in negative obstruction.(74)

Austria's golden opportunity to get involved in Polish affairs came at this time with the Julius Affair. Karl Baron Julius, an Austrian subject, lived in Warsaw where he earned his living as a gambler and a money-lender. During the Bavarian War, Julius offered his services to the Austrian ambassador to recruit deserters back to the colors. In reality, Julius did not restrict himself to Austrians but violated Polish law by enlisting anyone he could. With Stackelberg's approval, Polish authorities arrested Julius in October 1778. Stanisław August desired to treat the matter as quietly as possible in the hope of avoiding strained relations with Austria but Branicki and Lubomirski refused to try the case before the military tribunal and the marshal's court, respectively, so they would not have to bear responsibility. A special tribunal consisting of members of the previous diet was established which found Julius guilty. Although subject to the death penalty, Julius' punishment was moderated by the tribunal in deference to Austria and set as banishment from Poland and confiscation of his wealth. Nevertheless, the Austrian *chargé d'affaires,* de Caché, complained so vehemently that the Permanent Council demanded his recall without any effect.(75)

Austrian policy was designed to show how much trouble she could make for Russia in Poland. Ludwik Cobenzl, Austria's new **Ambassador** to Russia, arrived in Warsaw in the last days of 1779 while on his way to Petersburg determined to make a show of strength to revenge the Julius Affair. He prolonged his visit twice in order to draw demonstrations of loyalty from Polish subjects. Austria also cut off the revenues of Kazimierz Poniatowski from his estates in Austrian Galicia in order to put pressure on his brother, the king.(76)

Paradoxically, this show of force was aimed at bringing about closer relations between the two countries. Austrian-Russian relations improved sharply in the summer of 1780 with the meeting of Catherine and Joseph II at Mohilev. Joseph made a good impression on Catherine who invited him to Petersburg for the rest of the summer. Definite diplomatic negotiations on the ambassadorial level followed his return to Vienna. Successful conclusion of these negotiations led to a formal alliance for war against Turkey and had a profound effect on Polish internal politics.(77)

The proximity of Mohilev to Poland permitted royalists and op-positionists alike to pay homage to the Russian empress. Stanisław August once again sent his nephew, Prince Stanisław Poniatowski, as his personal representative with a letter of greeting for the Empress. Prince Stanisław also carried a letter for Potemkin requesting favors for Polish royalists. Verbal instructions permitted the Prince to sound out

Potemkin on the possibility of the Russian's accession to the ducal throne of Kurland, a Polish fief, in exchange for making Prince Stanisław his heir. The king warned his nephew to exercise great care in discussing politics and forbade him to mention the topic of succession to the Polish throne.(78)

Overwhelmed by a gracious reception, Prince Stanisław told Potemkin directly that the Polish king was willing to abandon hopes of arranging the Kurland ducal throne for the Poniatowski family and would support Potemkin for that position in exchange for his help in achieving a fundamental reform of the Polish government. At Potemkin's request, Poniatowski wrote a memorial asking for immediate return of distributive rights which the king had lost in 1775 as well as for measures to strengthen him further within the Permanent Council. He also requested for the indefinite future the establishment of an hereditary throne and the end of the unanimity rule in the diet. Prince Stanisław assured Potemkin that a reformed and strengthened Poland would remain loyal to Russia.(79) On hearing of his nephew's indiscretion, the usually calm Stanisław August was visibly outraged out of fear of total loss of the Russian Empress's favor or violent attack from the Opposition.(80)

Both Catherine and Josph displayed at Mohilev a desire to reduce factional strife in Poland between Royalists and the Opposition. Catherine paid no attention to Prince Stanisław's proposals and did not even reproach him for his ambitious hopes. Joseph responded coldly to the Polish nobles who made a show of enthusiasm for Austria, especially Prince Adam Czartoryski.(81) In return, Russia treated the Opposition in a friendly manner.Stackelberg once again turned to Austrian supporters in making up the Permanent Council for election by the 1780 diet allowing Branicki, Sapieha, Mierzejewski, Kurdwanowski, and Ignacy Potocki to remain in the Council for a second term.(82)

Russia's coldness to Stanisław August was particularly frustrating since he had had high hopes for further reform of his government to be achieved by a confederated diet. In a memorial presented to Stackelberg in early 1777, the king asked that a confederated diet be organized in 1778. The king repeated his request several months before the opening of the 1778 diet hoping that the threat of a Russo-Turkish war would convince Catherine that a confederation would be the best way to keep Poland quiet. Stackelberg refused, cheering the king only with the thought that, if war came, he would permit a confederated diet which would meet earlier than usual.(83)

The king circulated the usual letters in April 1778 asking senators for their opinions on the agenda for the diet. Replies showed that the Opposition had not given up despite its defeat in 1776. Leaders of the ministerial opposition demanded the withdrawal of Russian troops, prohibition of a confederated diet, abolition of the Permanent Council in favor of ministerial power, and reliance on the tradition *levée en masse* in case of war.(84)

Despite continued hostility to the king, the Opposition chose not to campaign actively at the 1778 dietines because Russian ambassador Stackelberg had already promised them political concessions. He had announced as well that Russia would permit no confederation to be formed.(85) The king paid the price of peace by assisting the election of some bitter enemies to the diet. Branicki's friend, Kurdwanowski, and Ignacy Potocki, for example, were elected at a dietine controlled by Józef Stępkowski, one of the king's lieutenants.(86)

Despite general royalist control, the dietines produced rather conservative instructions. Wołyń, Sandomierz, Podole, Kraków, and Czerniechów asked that no confederation be organized even though Stackelberg had already announced that there would be none. Kraków attacked the Permanent Council directly by instructing its deputies to ask that it cease "interpreting" the laws. Many dietines asked the postponement of consideration of the Zamoyski Law Code. Finally, Żmudź struck an interesting new note in its emphasis on Lithuanian separatist feeling. The dietine petitioned Stanisław August to restore the old custom of holding every third diet at Grodno, the Lithuanian capital, asked that he grant Lithuanians a proportionate number of places in the Royal Cadet School, and that the Lithuanian Military Commission be transferred from Warsaw to Grodno.(87)

Preparations completed, the 1778 diet opened in October under intense scrutiny to see whether this, the first "free" diet in the reign of Stanislaw August, would fall victim to the *liberum veto*. No one doubted that the veto was still in effect despite the sequence of confederated diets. The Fundamental Laws of 1768 stated precisely that the veto would "always remain in full force" so that any deputy had the power of "destroying the *activitatis* of business . . . orally or by written manifesto."(88) A Lithuanian deputy put these provisions into effect on the first day of the 1778. Disputing a procedural point, he threatened to suspend the diet entirely and walked out. Luckily, the protest was only symbolic and he returned soon so that the diet could continue.(89)

For the first time in fifty-two years, a free diet reached full term without "explosion" by the *liberum veto*.(90) Encouraged, Stanislaw August concluded that the Polish nobility had matured enough "to fear

. . . its dangerous prerogative''. Events proved the king correct. The *liberum veto* dropped out of use in all four succeeding free diets. Successful conclusion of the 1778 diet stabilized the regime psychologically. Polish nobles generally believed that neither the partition nor the constitutional revision of 1775-1776 were legally binding without confirmation by a free diet. While 1778 did not endorse these laws specifically, tacit acceptance sufficed.(91)

Unfortunately, elimination of the *liberum veto* did not solve all of Poland's legislative problems. The ever-present threat of its use prevented exercise of strong leadership from the diet's presiding officer.(92) Poles remained inordinately long-winded leading one Pole to remark that ''since the diet is free, the old ways have returned of speaking much and doing little''.(93) Another concluded in despair that Poles neither merit nor know how to use their liberty.(94) The Opposition used the traditional freedom of debate with great enthusiasm charging the marshal of the diet with suppressing debate and comparing the 1778 diet to the notorious ''silent diet'' *(sejm niemy)* of 1717 when deputies assented in silence to a humiliating Russian treaty. This accusation was so far from the truth that the marshal complained bitterly at the end of four weeks that the diet had ''neither enacted anything good nor revoked anything bad.''(95)

One fruitless debate took place when an opposition deputy submitted a bill to undo part of the 1776 law on the Permanent Council by stripping it of its power to interpret laws. The debates of the next few days featured attacks on the Council causing Stackelberg to intervene. He sent an official note asserting that the Opposition attacked an area of the Polish constitution guaranteed by the Russian empress. The Opposition gave in after making some attempt to find substitute phraseology.(96) In addition, the diet lost much time in attacks on the Lithuanian Treasury Commission for inaccuracies in its accounts. Tyzenhauz's lieutenant, Kazimierz Wolmar, blocked a full audit by threatening to prevent approval of the Crown Treasury Commission's books.(97)

These conditions made extremely difficult the passage of any substantive legislation, but the diet passed several minor bills. The king presented a program of seven ''propositions from the throne'' dealing with economic and administrative matters. Five of the seven were passed along with measures proposed from the floor. While failing to increase the size of the army, the diet declared that in 1780 it would treat the army as an ''economic matter'' which could be decided by majority rule. It increased the salary of the king's adjutant general, Jan Komarzewski, and the diet assumed financial responsibility for the

Royal Cadet School while assuring Lithuania that its sons would fill one-third of the vacancies. In addition to these decisions which were desired by the king, the diet limited him in his choice of diplomatic representatives to native-born nobles.(98)

Soon after the 1778 diet, Stanisław August began once again to request a confederation to introduce further reform. Stackelberg, dismayed at how effectively members of the Opposition resisted the king's plans in the Permanent Council, told him that he might permit a confederation in 1780. As a gauge of good faith, the ambassador and the king agreed on a marshal for that distant diet.(99)

While preparing for the 1780 diet, the king again expressed his desire for a confederated diet in order to ease the enactment of new taxes and approve the Zamoyski Law Code.(100) Despite what Stackelberg had said earlier, the Empress herself intervened to insist that "the *liberum veto* have its plain and whole effect at the coming diet.(101) Hence the 1780 diet, like its predecessor, was "free". In the hope of salvaging what he could, Stanisław August together with Stackelberg, attempted to conciliate the Opposition. They selected Antoni Malachowski, a popular and independent noble, as marshal of the diet and promised to make Branicki's nephew, Kazimierz Nestor Sapieha, Marshal of the Permanent Council. The king also promised to give Ignacy Potocki the first available ministry. Since the Opposition had been appeased, the dietines went quietly in October. Only one dietine was doubled. Nevertheless, most of the deputies received instructions against raising taxes.(102)

The second free diet of Stanisław August's reign opened October 2, 1780. The first sessions passed as usual in the selection of examining committees and elections to commissions for the next two years. The election of the king's nephew, Prince Stanisław Poniatowski, as Marshal of the Permanent Council came as a surprise because the king had promised to support Sapieha. Branicki and Lubomirski had betrayed Sapieha but the disappointed mother, Sapieżyna, held the king solely responsible for her son's defeat. Stanisław August may well have gone back on his word since his point of greatest consistence was support of his family and control of important political posts.(103)

Stanisław August fared poorly at the diet. The defeat of the Zamoyski Code and the indictment of Treasurer Tyzenhauz were major losses at a time when the diet also failed to deal with most of his propositions from the throne. Furthermore, the diet failed to increase the size of the army despite the enabling act of 1778 and was, incredibly, too busy to receive a present of a 300 man regiment from Szczęsny Potocki, a rich noble celebrating his first appearance at a diet. The only legislation of any significance passed was an appropriation for renovation of the decrepit fortress at Kamieniec Podolski and for the creation of a small arms factory. The National Education Commission was also extended for a second seven-year term and its members confirmed in office.(104)

At the end of the diet, Chancellor Onufry Okęcki praised the deputies for accomplishing ''the second complete free diet'' of the reign but acknowledged that ''the present diet, like the past one, cannot pride itself on the number of laws passed.(105) Stanisław August was bitterly discouraged. He called the parliamentary system worthless and bewailed the inability of Poles to realize that the unanimity rule prevented further reform.(106) Another observer, Julian Ursyn Niemcewicz, saw some cause for hope. He saw in the defeat of the Zamoyski Code the last act of national blindness and prejudice. But those qualities would ''quickly disappear before the spreading light of our new generation'' thanks to the education given by schools of the National Education Commission.(107)

CHAPTER IV

PARTY POLITICS

Stanisław August greeted the close of the 1780 diet with pleasure. He considered the political manoeuverings of the previous six weeks "an exercise in futility and irrationality" and "sustained himself by the thought that sooner or later some favorable crisis will arise which our country can profit from" to gain Russian approval for a confederated diet which would enact further reform.(1)

In Petersburg, the Empress Catherine regarded the peacefulness of the diet as a sign that she could finally withdraw her troops from Poland. Russia was happy to save the money spent on maintaining them abroad.(2) The Empress could be pleased with the pacification of Poland. In 1776, the prospect of withdrawing the Russian army inspired the Opposition with dreams of a *coup d'état*, but in 1780 no one noticed its exit. The peaceful atmosphere caused Russia to neglect Poland. Stackelberg was left for weeks without instructions or any funds as the College of Foreign Affairs virtually ceased activity.(3)

Much of Russia's indifference to Polish affairs stemmed from the conclusion in late spring 1781 of an alliance between Russia and Austria. Negotiations began in the summer of 1780 after Joseph II returned to Vienna from his trip to Russia and bore fruit after the death of Empress Maria Theresia in November. The two powers guaranteed Polish territorial integrity, reaffirmed the Treaty of Teschen ending the War of Bavarian Succession, and enacted a defensive alliance requiring each country to aid the other with an expeditionary corps consisting of 10,000 infantry and 2,000 cavalry. Secret supplementary letters specified that this agreement was aimed against the Ottoman Empire.(4)

One consequence of the new direction in foreign affairs adopted by Russia was the dismissal of Nikita Panin from command over Russian foreign affairs. Eased out on pretext of illness during the first half of 1781, Panin really lost his power because his pro-Prussian orientation made him unreliable under the new circumstances.(5) By 1782, Panin remained president of the College of Foriegn Affairs in name only. He no longer attended meetings, and foreign dignitaries were re-directed to vice-chancellor Ivan Ostermann. Ostermann himself was not a powerful figure, however, and authority passed into the hands of Alexander

Bezborodko, Catherine's secretary, who was elevated to the College of Foreign Affairs.(6) Despite personal enmity, Bezborodko cooperated fully with the greatest beneficiary of Panin's fall, Prince Grigorii Potemkin, Catherine's favorite and head of the War College, who desired Russia to expand southwards against the Turks. To this end, Potemkin engineered the loosening of ties with Prussia and the alliance with Austria.(7)

The Austro-Russian alliance greatly increased the difficulties of King Stanisław August since it meant an increase in the support given his opponents. The case of Baron Julius became a symbol of the new state of affairs in Poland. Julius had been arrested and convicted in 1778 for conducting recruiting operations in Poland. Russia now permitted Austria to reopen the case and instructed Stackelberg to treat with his Austrian colleague, Baron Franz Thugut on the issue "as with the minister of a friendly country."(8) The two ambassadors forced Stanisław August to reverse the verdict of Poland's highest court *(sad sejmowy)*concerning Julius's guilt and, in return, Austria accepted the king's calculations as to the size of the estate which would have to be returned to Julius as compensation.(9)

Prince Adam Czartoryski, who spent much of his time on his estates in Austrian Galicia, become the leader of the Opposition. Under pressure from Stackelberg, Stanisław August agreed to support Czartoryski's candidacy for Marshal of the Lithuanian Tribunal.(10) Czartoryski conducted himself as the model of rigorous justice showing no signs of partisanship. Many Polish nobles were very impressed, particularly since Czartoryski's conduct contrasted so sharply with the politically motivated decisions that the Tribunal had handed down when Tyzenhauz was in power. With popular support, Czartoryski hoped to become the Marshal of the next diet, but Stackelberg was not ready to grant an Austrian protege this much favor.(11)

Hetman Franciszek Branicki hoped to take advantage of Potemkin's rise through marriage with Alexandra Engelhardtova, officially Potemkin's niece, but reputed to be his daughter by the Empress Catherine.(12) Potemkin greeted him like royalty when Branicki came to Petersburg, but the wedding was delayed by the hetman's demand of a political price for going through with the ceremony — the return of the military prerogative taken away by the 1776 diet.(13) The wedding finally took place at the end of March amid great festivities. Catherine presented the couple with an enormous sum of money but no political concessions in Poland.(14) Concerned with developing the new Austrian alliance, however, Potemkin assured Stanislaw August by letter that Branicki would not cause trouble in the future and told Branicki in no uncertain terms that he fully supported Stackelberg.(15)

The future was not entirely bleak for Stanisław August who ingratiated himself with the Russian Grand Duke Paul, heir to the throne. Catherine sent her son on a trip to Western Europe in 1781 to prevent him from interfering with the negotiation of the treaty of alliance with Austria which Paul disapproved of.(16) Paul received orders from his mother to avoid Warsaw but Stanisław August arranged a reception at Wiśnowiec, the Lithuanian estate of the king's nephew-in-law, newly-appointed Crown Court Marshal, Michał Mniszech.(17) The Polish king acted as host. He brought cooks, musicians and his wine cellar to the meeting place at great expense.(18) Escorted by general Jan Komarzewski, the king's adjutant, and his nephew, Stanisław Poniatowski, Grand Duke Paul arrived at Wiśnowiec on October 31 bearing the pseudonym of *Comte du Nord* to avoid the irksome formalities of royal honors. Stanisław August, following Stackelberg's suggestion not to discuss politics, engaged in long conversations with the Grand Duke on neutral subjects and made a favorable impression. Opposed to his mother's policy and actions, Paul commented at one point that he was ashamed of Russia's in the partitions but Stanisław August replied that the Poles themselves were to blame.(19) The ducal couple went on to Vienna, Italy, and France accompanied by General Komarzewski as a sign of favor towards the Polish king. Grand Duke Paul desired to return to Russia via Warsaw, perhaps even to attend the approaching diet, but Catherine forbade him to visit either Prussia or Warsaw and ordered him to return by way of Prague and White Russia.(20)

Nevertheless, the Opposition continued to strengthen its resolve to attack Stanisław August sharply at the next diet. Prince Adam Czartoryski and Ignacy Potocki met frequently with the Austrian ambassador, Baron Franz Thugut while Joseph II showed special favor to Czartoryski by making him head of a newly-formed Galician Guards regiment.(21 The Austrian government moved to secure control over Polish nobles with estates in Galicia by commanding them to spend six months out of the year in Galicia or to pay a high tax. The decree clearly violated the 1775 treaty between Poland and Austria but Poland could do nothing.(22)

A dramatic incident permitted the Austrian ambassador to channel the activity of discontented Polish nobles into a strong attack on the royalist government.(23) Kajetan Sołtyk, Bishop of Kraków, who had been sent to Siberia by Russia for his opposition at the 1768 diet over the

Dissident question, returned to Poland after the first partition, broken in spirit.(24) Recalled to active life in 1781 in connection with a law suit over benefits between Hugo Kołłątaj and other clerics, Sołtyk attempted to regain control of his archdiocese from the Chapter of Cannons. The canons resisted and began to complain to the Permanent Council of Sołtyk's strange behavior, not the least of which was giving lavish public banquets and distributing gifts in order to buy the good will of the people of Kraków and threaten the Chapter with mob violence. The canons concluded that Sołtyk had gone mad and requested protection from the Permanent Council. At the king's urging, the Military Department ordered the commander of the Kraków garrison "to maintain the peace and security more closely among clerics and laity." He arrested the elderly bishop in the sacristy of the cathedral and, declaring him insane, imprisoned him. The Permanent Council sent a distinguished commission to Kraków to investigate but it reported in April that Sołtyk "has by God's will passed into such mental confusion that he can neither rule over his lands nor fulfill the obligations of a senator." The Council, therefore, removed Sołtyk to the bishop's palace in Kielce and his placed affairs under the control of four guardians, two chosen from his relatives and two from politically independent nobles. Bishop Garnysz, one of the members of the commission, in his clerical capacity, annulled the original decree imprisoning Sołtyk and punished the canons of the chapter with four weeks spiritual retreat and a 6000 Złoty fine to be given to charity. Sołtyk was given permission to return to Kraków when he regained his health. He never did.(25)

Hetman Seweryn Rzewuski, Sołtyk's fellow exile in Siberia, and several other members of the Permanent Council believed that Sołtyk's arrest was politically motivated. The arrest violated the basic Polish civil liberty, *neminem captivabimus*, which insured a trial of peers for nobles accused of offenses. He sent an angry letter of protest to the king and made speeches in the Permanent Council. Rzewuski and his friends paid little attention to an official rebuke from the Council for "improper expressions" contained in Rzewuski's letter of protest. The penalty of retreat and fine given the Chapter for acting hastily mollified them not at all.(26)

Stackelberg's attempts to restrain members of the Opposition failed and they spread baseless rumors that Bishop Michał Poniatowski, coadjutor of the Kraców diocese, had ordered Sołtyk's arrest to gain possession of the rich Krakow estates.(27) Encouraged by Austrian ambassador Thugut, the Opposition continually attacked alleged despotic aims of the Poniatowskis even though Stanisław Potocki, sent by the Opposition to investigate the affairs, admitted privately that "it is impossible to doubt that (Sołtyk) is not a little mad."(28)

Stanisław August appealed to Petersburg without success for help in restraining the Opposition's attacks on his government. Fearing that the Opposition would cast the first *liberum veto* of his reign, the king thought once again of organizing a confederated diet. In Petersburg, Polish minister, Antoni Deboli strongly seconded the effort since conversations with Hetman Branicki, who had not yet left Petersburg after his marriage, led him to the conclusion that a free diet would be stormy and unproductive.(29) Stanisław August sent his Court Marshal, Michał Mniszech, to St. Petersburg to argue his case for a confederated diet and to present proposals for strengthening the Permanent Council somewhat and changing treasury regulations. Mniszech made a good personal impression on the Russian court and gained Catherine's approval for his prospective promotion to Crown Great Marshal after the death of the aging Stanisław Lubomirski, but, not unexpectedly, the Empress refused to make any reforms or to allow the diet to be confederated. She explained, somewhat hypocritically, that she would need Prussia's and Austria's cooperation to organize a confederation and preferred to govern herself. As a result, Austrian partisans continued to make such attacks on the king that the diet was almost totally wasted.(30)

After an uneventful prelude, the diet of 1782 turned out to be the stormiest and least productive of all Polish "free" diets during the reign of Stanislaw August. The dietines were held without incident, and the diet opened calmly with the election of the king's candidate, Kazimierz Krasinski, as marshal. The usual elections to commissions occupied the first few sessions. Stackelberg showed good-will toward the king by preventing the Opposition from electing a single senator to the Permanent Council which ultimately contained no fewer than four of the king's relatives. The few Opposition deputies from the lower house who became members of the Council formed an insignificant minority.(31)

Reports delivered by the examining committees went smoothly until the review of the Permanent Council. The examining committee then read its report approving the Council's actions, but one member of the committee dissented and accused the Council of committing "the greatest . . . infringement" of the law possible in "seizing and imprisoning a free citizen and senator".(32) Several speakers tried to change the subject, but the rest of the day was spent in attacks on the Permanent Council for the arrest of Bishop Sołtyk.

The following day, Marshal Krasinski attempted to move to a

discussion of the Military Department but Karol Radziwiłł, who had returned from exile in 1778, denounced legislation which granted the army power to enforce court decrees on the grounds that it would exercise unrestrained and tyrannical authority. The chord once touched, Branicki was only too happy to present the arrest of Sołtyk as an example of unchecked tyranny. More deputies joined in vehement, acrimonious debate and introduced a number of bills which ran the gamut from approval to censure.(33)

Thanks to the king's intervention, the diet approved in general the activities of the Permanent Council for 1780-1782, by a vote of 135 to 34. Nevertheless, the Opposition continued to raise the Sołtyk question at every opportunity in succeeding days. Continual wrangling between supporters and opponents of the Permanent Council distressed the Marshal deeply. He complained that ''several days have passed (and) I have to admit with sorrow that . . . they have (generally) passed completely uselessly,'' adding that ''this is already our third free diet but what good does it do us when we are accomplishing nothing.''(34)

The Sołtyk issue came to a vote once again in the lower house of the Polish diet as rival bills were submitted by Royal Party and the Opposition to overrule the arrest of Sołtyk by the Permanent Council. Instead of considering the bills as a whole, the diet took each point separately in a long debate. The Opposition lost on each by similar margins. Significantly, however, they exercised their right to request a secret ballot where the king's margin declined substantially (on point one it declined from 131-38 to 98-67).(35) This showed that many royalists followed the king only to take advantage of the patronage which he dispensed. The Senate also rejected the Opposition's bill.

The Opposition's objections overcome at long last, the diet could get down to work on the king's legislative program which included a request for funds to search for new sources of salt, increase in the number of Lithuanian senators, and some minor army reforms.(36) But it was too late. The diet had reached its last working day. Marshal Krasinski could only say that ''what we have achieved covers scarcely several pages . . . but at least we should find some consolation in that we will leave no traces . . . of the injuries which we have inflicted on the country.(37) Stanisław August expressed the fear that the future diets would follow the bad example set by the Opposition's filibuster and that Poland would decline towards final destruction.(38)

The freedom of the Opposition to spend the entire time of the diet on attacks on the king's government stemmed from their support by Russia and Austria. The king bitterly offended Stackelberg before the diet by refusing to grant sufficient patronage to some of the ambassador's favorites. When Thugut offered his support, Stackelberg agreed "to look the other way . . . to avoid seeing the Kraków matter."(39) After a period of indulgence, however, Stackelberg put an end to the Opposition's attacks. He assembled Opposition deputies in the fourth week of the diet to tell them that "the empress does not permit the creation of factions and parties in Poland" and stated the same to Thugut in somewhat more elegant language. Nevertheless, the ambassador refused the king's request for a confederation.(40)

Austria had a concrete financial interest in fomenting discontent at the Polish diet. She hoped to prevent passage of the king's proposal to search actively for salt on Polish territory in order to replace the mines at Wieliczka which Poland had lost to Austria in the first partition. Austria intended to retain her revenues from export of salt to Poland.(41)

The Opposition, however, did not act merely as an Austrian puppet. Each deputy had his own reasons for paralyzing the already slender power of the diet. Stanisław Potocki had asked Stanisław August for his support in the elections to the Permanent Council. The king refused with a gentle reminder of Potocki's past opposition.(42) Similarly, the king had refused Ignacy Potocki's request for Tyzenhauz's ministerial post, which was not yet even vacant.(43) The hetmen Branicki and Seweryn Rzwuski joined the Potockis (Marshal Lubomirski was too old and feeble by this time to play an active role) in Opposition. Branicki attempted to act as the Russian empress's representative in Poland telling the deputies to the diet that Catherine desired them to protect poor Bishop Sołtyk. When drunk, he also told the king that he would be forced to abdicate within a half year. Rzewuski warned that "the terrible fate of the Prince Bishop of Kraków angers us all and warns everyone that the same might happen to him." He also told Stanisław August to beware "for the Polish nobility is not the German nobility", and, mixing metaphors and countries, reminded him of the fate of Charles I of England.(44)

The 1782 diet failed because of the perfect coordination of events: Stackelberg was angry about patronage and Thugut concerned about salt revenues while the magnates looked for a chance to humiliate the king. Finding an issue close to the heart of Poland's Golden Freedoms, the Opposition gained a measure of public acceptance, although ballotting showed how small a measure they won. Except for the elections to the various commissions and approval of their actions for the previous two years (plus ratification of minor border rectifications with Russia), no legislation passed at all. Stanisław August, who had hoped to pass an eight point program featuring salaries for deputies at the diet, reflected ruefully that "we have not seen so stormy a diet in Poland for many years."(45)

Looking at the failure of the 1782 diet, one foreign observer concluded that

The King of Poland has lost the Confidence of his subjects . . . In the distant provinces, the Minds of the People are totally estranged from Him. Should Russia withdraw her Protection from His Polish Majesty or so far engage elsewhere as not to be able to support him with her troops, a Revolution in this country is much to be apprehended."(46)

Though this may have described much of the nobility, more discerning observers saw great power intrigues. Deboli reported from Petersburg that Russia was too interested in maintaining her alliance with Austria to resent that country's role during the Diet. Vice-chancellor Ostermann told Deboli that Austria had a right to protect her interest on the salt issue, but promised to support Stanislaw August actively in 1784. He assured Deboli that the king would have a free hand in the selection of senators and members of the Permanent Council. Ostermann even guaranteed that the Austrian Party's influence would decline in the course of the next two years.(47)

Luckily for the Polish court, the Austrian party weakened quickly after the 1782 diet. Marshal Lubomirski looked older and feebler every day as his death approached; Austrian ambassador Thugut attended his bedside constantly. Lubomirski died in 1783, not long after August Czartoryski whose authority had remained great despite his inactivity. With their deaths, the Opposition lost more than leaders. Lubomirski's widow refused to spend the large sums on politics that her husband had.(48) The one individual who could fill the gap left by their deaths, Prince Adam Czartoryski, having entered Austrian service, spent so much time with the Galician guard that many nobles looked on him as having surrendered his Polish citizenship. Czartoryski explained that he had accepted Joseph II's invitation to become head of the Galician guard in order to help keep Galician youth Polish expressing satisfaction at working in "Europe" rather than under the "barbarous, asian" muscovite rule in Poland.(49)

Early in 1783, Prince August Sułkowski went to Peterburg to offer his remedy for the unruly diet of 1782. Deboli, who disliked Sułkowski intensely, tried to block the mission but Stanisław August could not prevent him from going. The king, however, asked him to keep in close touch with Deboli and not to act too independently. The king also instructed Deboli not to interfere with Sułkowski. En route to Russia, Sułkowski stopped at Białocerkiew where he received assurance from Branicki that he would not raise the issue of Bishop Sołtyk at the 1784 diet. Branicki was on the defensive since marital troubles with his Russian wife made him unpopular in Petersburg.(50)

Sułkowski arrived in Petersburg with a plan for a Permanent Diet, similar in design to his ideas of 1773, which would meet not just six weeks every second year but could be in session whenever necessary. This diet, he specified, would meet under the aegis of a general confederation and would enact an alliance with Russia and Austria. The diet would also impose new taxation to make possible the enlargement of the army to the legal limit, 30,000 men, as well as train a "national militia" of 75,000 men. Deboli considered these plans premature and the king, when he heard, was outraged at Sułkowski's audacity. Militarily, the king considered a militia useless against regular troops and politically, he felt it gave Austria too much influence. Deboli nonetheless arranged for Sułkowski to present his plan to Ostermann who promised to inform the empress. His promise was only politeness; Russia entertained no ideas of constitutional change in Poland. Stackelberg had shown his disapproval of Sułkowski's ideas as well.(51)

Stanisław August disapproved of Sułkowski's initiative but he entertained similar ideas and changes in European relations suddenly left him in a position to offer his own plans for reform. After nine years of uncertain control over the Crimea, Empress Catherine II decided to annex it to Russia in April 1783. Turkey called this a violation of the Treaty of Kuckuk-Kainardji and considered going to war.(52) Stanisław August thought of gaining permission to enact reform in exchange for an offer to give assistance to Russia in case of war. More interested in finding a way to handle the 1784 diet than in fighting a war against Turkey, he waited many months before presenting his plans.

In late May 1783, the Marshal of the Permanent Council asked members to stay close to Warsaw instead of returning to their estates for the summer, so that the Council could assemble in case war broke out between Russia and Turkey. Poland, herself, seemed close to war with Turkey when Turks near Kamieniec Podolski fired on Polish soldiers mistaking their uniforms for Russian. Rumors began to circulate that Frederick II was formulating plans for another partition of Poland. Austria's renewed insistence that Galician Poles reside six months on their Galician estates seemed to indicate to the king that Austria would agree to another partition.(53)

In January 1784, Stanisław August finally proposed to Russia that an alliance be signed between the two countries and ratified in Poland by a confederated diet which would also enact domestic reforms. The king desired a ''defensive and perpetual alliance which would assure a permanent existence to my country and make it invulnerable to attack.'' Russia would gain sure control of the entire Polish kingdom through the alliance without war or expense; Austrian and Prussian intrigues, like those which produced the first partition, would no longer be possible. Stanisław August attempted to convince Catherine that Russian self-interest would lead her to permit reform of the Polish administration, finances, and army. He did not send Deboli any text of a proposed treaty. He hoped only for agreement in principle. In the event of failure to gain an alliance, Stanisław August selected a fat consolation prize for himself — payment of his huge debt.(54)

Stackelberg agreed that a confederation would be very useful for managing the 1784 diet but he refused to intervene in Petersburg since he knew Catherine's belief that confederations are ''a political, violent disease'' and a ''convulsive and painful state for the nation.'' He did, however, promise to support Stanisław August in his attempt to get Russian permission for raising the debt issue. In Petersburg, Deboli tried to convince Ostermann that a free diet would be useless, but his arguments fell on deaf ears. The Russian court continued to fear that the formation of a confederation would cause great unrest in Poland. Thus Deboli ceased to discuss the possibility of forming an alliance with Russia and concentrated on securing a letter restraining Branicki from attacking the Permanent Council as he had in 1782(55)

The king had little to worry about since the Opposition had shown little activity since the 1782 diet. Stanisław August hoped to mollify Branicki's nephew, Prince Kazimierz Nestor Sapieha, by granting him permission to buy a rich estate in Lithuania in exchange for Sapieha's promise not to use his influence against him. Sapieha honored his promise at the 1784 dietines, although he announced his desire to become Marshal of the Permanent Council. Branicki importuned Seweryn Rzewuski and Ignacy Potocki to work with him at the 1784 diet in opposition to the king, but they refused for lack of Austrian support.(56)

Stanisław August gained new support from the rich Lithuanian magnate, Szczęsny Potcki, who, alone of the Potocki family, remained on good terms with the king. Potocki acted as an intermediary in a delicate law case involving a royalist and member of the Opposition and, in return for his help, received permission to choose the deputies at his local dietine.(57) The king also consulted with his nephew-in-law, Ludwik Tyszkiewicz and his chief agent in Lithuania, Joachim Chreptowicz, about the dietines. Newly-named Marshal Kazimierz Raczyński handled most of the king's affairs in Wielkopolska. The king appeared to be on good terms with Stackelberg, who pledged himself to support the king fully in order to make up the loss of Andrzej Mokronowski, who had just died.(58)

After thorough preparation — and in the absence of any open dispute with the Opposition — the dietines went almost entirely to the royal party. Trouble erupted only in Podole where three nobles died in a clash between Branicki's friends and royalists. The dietine went to the Opposition which selected, among others, Prince Adam Czartoryski as deputy. The Wolyń dietine, however, which had often been a stronghold of the Opposition, elected royalist deputies and enacted only one instruction which might be construed as hostile to the king — namely, that no confederation be organized.(59)

Although Polish law required that one of every three diets be held in Lithuania, it had been many years since the diet had been held outside of Warsaw. Lithuanian deputies demanded in 1782 that the law be honored but Russia advised against transfer of the diet on the grounds that if it underwrote the king's expenses by approving his loan, he should not increase them sharply by travelling.(60) The king thought the idea of holding the diet in Grodno "painful, disagreeable, and costly", but he had Deboli explain to the Russian court that the law left him no choice.(61)

To gain fullest advantage from the situation, Stanisław August made a long, circuitous trip through Lithuania to visit nobles in hope of winning new support. The king left Warsaw on August 26 in the company of Bishop Naruszewicz, General Komarzewski, and a large party. The day was festive; crowds gathered along the streets of Warsaw and nearby villages to watch the procession.(62) During his journey, Stanisław August visited Lithuanian Chancellor Aleksander Sapieha at Różana and Hetman Michał Ogiński at Slonim. The highpoint of the trip was Nieświeża, where Karol Radziwiłł gave the king a magnificent welcome. Stanisław August paid careful attention to the lesser nobility along the way because he knew how deeply many distrusted him for his foreign ways and foreign advisors. Tact and graciousness won Stanisław August many friends. He proved that he respected Polish canons of equality among nobles.(63) Reaching Grodno a few days before the opening of the diet, Stanisław August had news of the death of Primate Tomasz Ostrowski in Paris. A special meeting of the Permanent

Council raised the king's brother, Bishop Michał Poniatowski, to this highest position in the Polish Church.(64)

In order to prevent a repetition of the Opposition attacks of 1782, Russia had decided to assist Stanisław August's preparations for the 1784 diet. Potemkin wrote Branicki personally to this effect and Seweryn Rzewuski received similar instructions from his mother-in-law, Lubomirska, who had heard from Stackelberg. These two nobles chose to remain at home rather than attend a diet which would give no play to their obstructionist abilities.(65) Kazimierz Sapieha and Ignacy Potocki threatened in private to cast a *liberum veto* to prevent passage of the king's debt bill, but Stackelberg dissuaded them by threatening them with the empress's displeasure.(66)

Before giving up, the Opposition succeeded in adding to its ranks Szczęsny Potocki, the richest man in Poland, who was piqued at Stanisław August, for failing to pay enough attention to him while travelling to Grodno.(67) Potocki's defection from the royalist camp took on added significance from the popularity which he won through the gift to the Republic of a 400 man regiment and twenty-four cannon. The regiment was to be stationed on Potocki's estates and would guard that portion of the Russian border. The Military Department of the Permanent Council exercised military command, at least in theory, even though Potocki could choose the officers. Kazimierz Sapieha, Lithuanian Artillery General, shared the triumph with the gift of twelve cannon.(68)

Freed from Opposition attacks, Stanisław August chose a Permanent Council according to his wishes excluding Opposition leaders who had life so difficult in the past. Most of the new councillors were young, relatively unknown, and loyal to the king, having grown up in his service.(69) Two measures passed were costly. The king brought some relief to the condition of his disgraced former lieutenant, Antoni Tyzenhauz. Feeling that enough time had passed to allow passions to cool, particularly in view of the Treasurer's physical and mental collapse, Stanisław August asked that the triple damages, which the Lithuanian Treasury Commission required him to pay, be rescinded. The diet agreed after some debate. Most important, the diet gave Stanisław August 4,000,000 zlp. towards payment of his debts.(70)

Two measures were passed to increase Polish trade with Russia: a reduction of Polish tariffs in the Ukraine and an agreement to reduce the duty on Polish exports shipped to or through Riga. Another law granted a charter for the Black Sea Company, organized in 1782 by Prot Potocki, and appointed him Polish consul in Cherson to assist its operations. The Permanent Council was instructed to ask Austria to relax restrictions on mixed subjects and to make minor corrections in the Silesian border with Prussia.(71)

Important domestic measures were also discussed. The diet passed a law setting out in great detail the process for using the army to execute court decrees. The army came in for reform. Offcers were refused permission to sell commissions until after fifteen years of service, a measure which gave the king greater control over appointment of officers. Finally, the king succeeded in gaining citizenship for two princes desirous of entering his service; the Prince Frederick of Anhalt-Koeton and the Prince Charles of Nassau-Siegen.(72)

Despite several minor Opposition outbursts, the 1784 diet became the most successful free diet of Stanisław August's reign. In numerical terms, more legislation passed here than at any other free diet. The average number of bills passed at the 1778, 1780, 1782, and 1786 diets was 26, while the 1784 diet passed forty-six laws. More bills might yet have been passed if Stackelberg had not rejected the king's request for a three-week extension of the diet.(73) In quality, too, the 1784 diet distinguished itself at least by the low standards of interpartition diets. Russia, of course, permitted no constitutional change nor would the Poles themselves raise taxes. Nevertheless, enough worthwhile measures were passed to disprove the harsh judgment expressed by Saxony's envoy, Essen, who said that "the twenty year reign of King Stanisław August made that country fall deeper into demoralization instead of improving it."(74) The greatest benefit was drawn by the king, personally, however.

CHAPTER V

TRIUMPH OF THE OPPOSITION

Stackelberg congratulated himself on the tranquility of the 1784 diet; he considered it a major breakthrough in his pacification of Poland. Polish envoy Deboli was also pleased but he feared the experience would confirm Russia's determination to hold all diets as free diets. While admitting that the 1784 diet passed some worthwhile legislation, Deboli still maintained that only a change in the constitution would cure the serious problems afflicting Poland.(1) The French observer, Bonneau, who had expected the diet to be as fruitless as its predecessor, was greatly impressed by the harmony of the diet. He reported to Versailles that Stanisław August had at long last achieved a true reconciliation with the Polish nobility.(2)

The Dogrumowa Affair soon showed that conflict betweeen the king and the Opposition had not abated. Anna Maria Dogrumowa, a Dutch-born adventuress, had come to Warsaw in the 1770's and took up with different men. Left without support around 1780, she approached the Polish court in hope of reward with invented tales of plots on the king's life by important nobles like Adam Czartoryski and Antoni Tyzenhauz. After three years of fruitless attempts, Dogrumowa reversed her system and went to Czartoryski with the story that Ferdynand Ryx, the king's chamberlain, and General Jan Komarzewski, were planning to kill him. In order to prove her claim, Dogrumowa brought Ryx to her chambers on the pretext of reporting yet another plot against the king, but conducted the conversation so skillfully that Count Stanisław Potocki and an English merchant named Taylor thought they heard Ryx make arrangements to kill Czartoryski. The two eavesdroppers rushed in from the next room, seized Ryx, and took him to Marshal Michal Mniszech, who was in charge of justice in the capital, Mniszech, although a royalist, had no choice but to confine Ryx. He also put Dogrumowa under loose house arrest in the palace of the Marshal Lubomirski's widow.(3)

This spectacular *affaire* stunned Warsaw; everyone rushed to take sides. The royal party, of course, believed Ryx and Komarzewski innocent, while the Opposition proclaimed them guilty. Some openly laid blame on higher officials like Michał Poniatowski, the king's brother,

Stanisław Poniatowski, his nephew, or Michał Mniszech, his nephew-in-law. Branicki accused his military rival, General Komarzewski.(4) In any case, the Opposition put Stanisław August's reputation on trial since he bore the responsibility for choosing his close associates.

Stanisław August saw the Dogrumowa affair as part of a campaign by the Opposition to achieve power. Before the 1784 diet, Prince Adam Czartoryski had announced the betrothal of his daughter to Prince Ludwig of Wurtemberg, brother of Russian Grand Duchess, Maria Feodorovna, and an officer in the army of Frederick II. Personally, Ludwig had little to recommend him since he fell continually into debt, but the Russian empress, Catherine, hoping to gain influence over Czartoryski, guaranteed the prospective bridegroom's financial prospects.(5) Nevertheless, Catherine grew to suspect that Czartoryski aimed at gaining the Polish throne for himself or his son-in-law in alliance with the Prussian and Austrian courts. She ordered Stackelberg to watch developments closely and authorized him to intervene with the Austrian authorities if they appeared to be supporting Czartoryski.(6)

The Austrian attaché in Warsaw, de Caché, took advantage of the Dogrumowa affair to rally supporters to the Austrian cause. He immediately informed Stackelberg of Austria's deep concern that Adam Czartoryski receive justice from the court which was about to convene and de Caché intervened with diplomatic notes at every step of the proceedings henceforth.(7) Vienna contacted Petersburg as well to settle the dispute by some compromise by-passing the Polish authorities even though the Emperor Joseph did not believe the truth of Czartoryski's charge. Russia refused as Stackelberg convinced his sovereign that it would be improper "for the names of two great sovereigns to appear in this miserable intrigue."(8) To keep pressure on the Polish authorities, Austria renewed the Julius affair by questioning the amount of compensation which Poland had paid, a violation of Thugut's agreement with Stackelberg.(9)

The Russian court failed to understand how the affair undermined royal prestige and refused to help Stanisław August against his enemies. Ostermann told Deboli that he believed Ryx innocent but could not understand why the king feared the publicity surrounding the affair. Fully six weeks after Ryx's arrest, Stackelberg tried to mediate the matter but defeated his own purpose by admitting that he had no orders from the empress. Thus, Stackelberg had protected the king against Austria but forced him to fight his own battles against the Opposition.(10)

Court proceedings began in January 1785. The judges, selected from both members of the Opposition (including Ignacy Potocki, brother of the leading prosecution witness) and royalists, heard conflicting testimony from the principals, Ryx, Dogrumowa, Stanislaw Potocki, and Taylor. In order to resolve the question, the court turned to the rules of evidence which resulted in the dismissal of testimony from all prosecution witnesses. Stanisław Potocki's testimony was barred on the grounds that he was a close relative of Czartoryski's (nephew-in-law). Taylor spoke little French and could not be trusted to have understood the conversation between Ryx and Dogrumowa. Evidence given by the Russian major Ogrumov, Dogrumowa's husband from whom she was separated, tended to discredit Dogrumowa's reliability as a witness.(11) As a result, the court acquitted Ryx who immediately filed a counter-suit against Dogrumowa and Taylor which led to a sentence of life imprisonment and branding for Dogrumowa and six months for Taylor. Stackelberg protested the brutal treatment accorded Dogrumowa but the king and Mniszech told him it was too late to change the sentence. Stanisław Potocki received a slight reprimand and Adam Czartoryski was fined for bringing false accusations.(12)

A pamphlet war kept the Dogrumowa affair before the public even after the court had handed down its verdict. Stanisław August commissioned Bishop Adam Naruszewicz to prepare a long book based on court records which appeared in print before the end of the year.(13) The Opposition was even more active, since the verdict had gone against it. "First Real Explanation about the Trial of the Prince General of Podole" accused the king of managing the entire defense. The author also accused Maurice Glaire, appointed court translator, of forcing Dogrumowa to incriminate herself by means of threats.(14) An "impartial Pole" observed that the public had a right to expect Ryx's conviction since the evidence was overwhelming and Ryx's "terror and hopelessness" before the trial showed his guilt. The Tribunal acquitted Ryz by prosecuting the "form" of the accusation instead of the "substance".(15)

The Opposition presented its official version of the Dogrumowa affair in a book written by Stanisław Potocki but published anonymously. Potocki asked his readers to examine the evidence (which appeared here in the form of letters from a son in Warsaw to his father in the provinces) impartially and felt confident that they would find consistent "hidden partisanship" in the actions of the judges.(16) The Opposition also commissioned the noted French pamphleteer, Simon Linguet, who was then living in England, to write on the trial. The Polish envoy in London dissuaded him. Michał Poniatowski failed to convince his cousin "as a close relative, a compatriot, and a minister of peace", to submit to the verdict of the court. The king's appeal to family feeling also failed. Czartoryski's sister, the widow of Marshal Lubomirski, also left Poland and lived out the remainder of her days in Paris.(18) Before her departure, however, Lubomirska made a show of friendship towards Taylor by visiting him frequently in jail.(19)

Adam Czartoryski reached Vienna in early April 1785 determined to stay in Austria, despite an unsympathetic reception accorded to him by Joseph II, and not to take any further role in Polish politics.(20) Stanisław August sent his nephew, Stanisław Poniatowski, to dissuade Prince Adam from this course. After twice refusing, Czartoryski finally agreed to receive his young cousin but rejected reconciliation. Prince Adam left shortly thereafter for western Europe, embarrassed by Joseph's continual barbed comments. The Austrian ruler, like Stanisław August, attempted to convince Czartoryski to pay the fine levied by the Polish court, but Prince Adam refused. Observers concluded that he intended to return to Poland after all and would reopen the case at the 1786 diet.(21)

Hetman Franciszek Branicki took advantage of continued public interest in Dogrumowa by claiming that the presence of his name on the court decree settling that case slandered him. His charges, as usual, were completely without foundation since the decree specifically cleared him of allegations made by Dogrumowa. Branicki wrote to the Russian Empress requesting her support in removing his name from the court decree and began to gather Polish supporters for the next diet.(22) Russia decided to appease the hetman in the belief that he was honestly upset by the court decree.(23) Thus, Branicki's lieutenant, Kajetan Kurdwanowski, could say in Warsaw society, without inviting reproach from the Russian ambassador, that the court decree had wronged Branicki and that the 1786 diet would be stormy if Branicki's demands were not met. Branicki himself stated publicly that he had Russian permission to raise the matter in the diet.(24)

Early in the spring of 1786, the Opposition began its preparations for the diet. Ignacy Potocki, Kazimierz Sapieha, and Franciszek Branicki met at Siedlce for several weeks to lay plans for the diet while enjoying the lavish hospitality of Hetman Ogiński's wife.(25) Ignacy and Stanisław Potocki spread word that Potemkin would help them elect members of the Opposition to the Permanent Council even if Stackelberg supported the king. Branicki and Ignacy Potocki convinced Adam Czartoryski, who had returned to Poland, that Stanisław August planned to attack him at the diet and that Czartoryski had to act to protect himself.(26)

Czartoryski rejoined the Opposition and contributed heavily to its campaign chest.(27) To woo the lesser nobility, Czartoryski invited five hundred guests to his palace at Puławy to see a performance of the play ''The Spartan Mother'' with his wife and children playing the lead roles. Franciszek Kniaźniń's play described patriotism in the ancient world and the need for a proper civic upbringing. The spectators understood this as an allusion to Polish traditions of ''Sarmatian'' virtues and responded with''emotional involvement and truly national civil enthusiasm.''(28)

As soon as Stanisław August learned that Branicki intended to reopen the Dogrumowa case at the diet, he pressed the Russian court to restrain the hetman as it had in 1784. Deboli seemingly won the support of Catherine's secretary, Alexander Bezborodko, but his promises of help proved empty. Vice-chancellor Ostermann promised Deboli an imperial letter restraining Branicki but admitted several months later, that he had sent orders to Stackelberg to support Branicki's attempt to change court decree.(29)

The Polish king gained his usual large majority at the provincial dietines in early September but the Opposition showed great strength in Lithuania. The political successors to Treasurer Antoni Tyzenhauz, Joachim Chreptowicz at the head, showed themselves unwilling to spend enough money in bribes and expense money for supporters to control the dietines. The Opposition, aware, of the deficiencies, resolved to take up the slack. Kazimierz Sapieha campaigned for six months in the district of Brześć-Litewski. His supporters outnumbered the royalists by a margin of two to one. Adam Czartoryski brought his wife and children dressed in Polish costume to the dietine in Łuck and also imported armed retainers from other districts. Prince Sanguszko, the king's agent, tried to reach a compromise splitting the representation half and half, but Czartoryski would not agree. The result was a doubled dietine. The same situation prevailed at Żytomierz where Branicki refused a compromise offered by Józef Stępkowski, acting for the king. The several thousand supporters whom Branicki brought to the dietine elected five oppositionist and Stępkowski's son. The Opposition also captured several other dietines.(30)

The 1786 diet met once again in Warsaw. The Opposition attempted from the beginning to create confusion. To show their objection to certain procedural irregularities, members of the Opposition rushed out of their seats, ran to the center of the chamber, shouted, blew out the candles, and refused to let the secretary proceed with the agenda. Since it was eight o'clock the Marshal adjourned the session, but Opposition deputies remained behind to elect their own marshal.(31) Two days passed with the diet in adjournment but when the deputies returned, some bore arms. A compromise reached the following day permitted a solution of the doubled dietines despite Hetman Rzewuski's attempt to rally the Opposition to further defiance. The Wołyń royalists withdrew their claims to seats at the diet while oppositionists from Podole similarly resigned themselves. This did not prevent the Opposition from shouting angrily during elections or stop their leaders, Branicki, Ignacy Potocki and Szczesny Potocki, from presenting a manifesto denouncing the temporary presiding officers for refusing to permit a second ballot. Similar controversy surrounded the vote on the doubled Wilno delegation. The diet finally concluded preliminaries with the election of Stefan Gadomski, a member of the Russian party, as Marshal.(32)

Elections to the Permanent Council proceeded smoothly, probably because some of the most prominent royalists had withdrawn. Only one oppositionist was elected, however. When the time came to select judges for the assessorial court, however, the Opposition refused to leave their nomination to the king, the usual practice. Elections by secret ballot took two days.(33)

Stanisław August anticipated the Opposition in the matter of the Dogrumowa affair by introducing a measure designed to satisfy Branicki's complaints. The diet instructed interested parties to draw up a final text in private. Ignacy Potocki (acting for Adam Czartoryski), Branicki, Stackelberg, and Stanislaw August took almost two weeks to find an acceptable formula which was then read in both chambers of the diet. But the king was astonished to find an essential phrase altered. Two more days of negotiations were required to reach agreement.(34)

The diet settled the Dogrumowa case by passing two resolutions. First, all citizens were enjoined to forget the case entirely so that the affair would be treated ''as if it had not taken place.'' The courts were forbidden to release any documents pertaining to it. Dogrumowa, the principal actor, remained in prison. A second resolution specifically cleared Czartoryski, Branicki, and Tyzenhauz of any suspicion which the decree and the proceedings might have cast on them. Czartoryski did not have to pay his fine.(35)

Military affairs stirred strong debate in the diet and underscored the gulf between the king and the Opposition. The latter attacked the Military Department for its proposed regulation reducing the number of semi-professional noble cavalrymen serving in the army while increasing full-time regulars who were subject to rigorous discipline. A number of speakers accused the king of seeking to undermine the patriotism of Polish nobles by preventing them from serving in the army. Branicki denounced Komarzewski as the one bearing responsibility for the regulation. Referring to rumors that Komarzewski was not of noble birth, Branicki claimed that he failed to understand Polish traditions. (In fact, he had been secretly ennobled in 1781). Finally, the diet repealed the regulation and reestablished the *status quo* of 1775-76 with its high proportion of ill-disciplined, part-time, noble cavalry. The diet also rejected the king's plan to create specialist officers (General of the Cavalry, Infantry, Quartermaster) in order to prevent the king from appointing his supporters to those posts.(36)

The Opposition contested as well a regulation which seemed to open the possibility of foreign nobles serving in the Polish army. Several speakers expressed concern that Poles would be driven abroad if their places at home were filled. This attack was intended as a reproach to Stanisław August for employing the Prince of Nassau-Siegen, a naturalized Polish citizen, to direct royal supporters at one of the Lithuanian dietines. When the diet refused to permit anyone but native-born nobles from serving in the Polish army, Nassau entered the service of the Russian empress and attended her during her voyage to Crimea in 1787.(37) The tactic of appealing to patriotism did more than deprive Stanislaw August of a supporter, it brought an explosion of nationalist sentiment, even involving royalist deputies, which foreshadowed the Four Years Diet. Hetman Branicki, himself willing to see two foreign officers in each regiment, feared to speak out against total exclusion of foreigners.(38)

The attack on the army led to a general offensive against the Permanent Council. Prince Sapieha blamed that institution for the inefficacy of post-partition diets. He claimed that the Council made so many mistakes and committed such injustices that there was simply not enough time to consider them all, let alone debate new legislation. Several days later, Sapieha called for the abolition of the Permanent Council altogether and return to the old system of government. Such a strong attack echoed Szczęsny Potocki's request for protection of dietines against outside interference, a measure which would have permitted local magnates to use force, but refused the king the means to counter it.(39) Potocki also complained that the king undermined Polish liberties by choosing the marshal of the diet six months before the diet instead of leaving free choice to the deputies. Ironically, this permitted the king to refuse a request by Szczęsny Potocki's son to serve as the marshal in 1788.(40)

Overall, the diet of 1786 was not as bad as the 1782 diet since some legislation passed. Nevertheless, it represented a significant defeat for both the king and the country. Polish diets met so seldom and for such short periods that their failure to enact any quantity of legislation condemned the country to further stagnation. Although three of the king's propositions from the throne passed, the other seven were without exception of economic and military benefit. Passing them would entailed no political disadvantage to the Opposition. The attacks of the Opposition so aggrieved Stanisław August that he suspended publication of the parlimentary record.(41)

Maurice Glaire wrote to Stanisław August's agent in Paris, General Monet, with relief that at last "this scandalous diet" had come to an end. He accused the Opposition of personal selfishness and lack of concern for the common good.(42) Another western European, the French observer, Bonneau, expressed amazement at the ability of the small number of opposition deputies to paralyze the diet. Stanisław August, he reported, had given way on many issues to avoid even worse scenes than had actually taken place.(43)

The Opposition continued its resolve after the diet. Prince Adam Czartoryski, while forced by Austria to come to Warsaw to thank the king for striking his name from the Dogrumowa court decree, arranged for a gathering of Opposition leaders at his estate in Puławy. Branicki, Szczęsny Potocki, and a considerable number of lesser nobles met in mid-December in an impressive show of strength. The highlight of their convention was another performance of "The Spartan Mother" featuring Adam Czartoryski's family as actors.(44)

After the diet, Stanisław August began to think once again of gaining Russia's permission for a major step forward in Polish reform. Catherine II had let it be known before the 1786 diet that she intended to tour the newly-acquired territory of the Crimea. Stanisław August saw this as an opportunity to press once again, as he had in 1783-84, for a military alliance with Russia which would give Poland some weight in the European state system and which, for it to be useful to Russia, would require further internal reform. Since Catherine's route would take her near the eastern borders of Poland, the king immediately applied for permission to meet her and, towards the end of the diet, received word that she had agreed.(45) The king quickly sent his advisor, General Komarzewski, to Petersburg to make arrangements. Catherine generously promised to devote considerable time to the Polish king if he met her in Kiev. Komarzewski reluctantly admitted that Polish law forbade the king to leave Polish soil without specific authorization from the diet. Since calling an extraordinary diet was out of the question,

Stanisław August could meet only Catherine as she travelled down the Dniepr by boat.(46)

Stanisław August left Warsaw in late February 1787 in the company of Stackelberg, whom the empress had ordered to meet her. Members of the royal party also included the king's nephews, Stanisław and Józef Poniatowski.(47) After a month on muddy roads, the king reached the Ukrainian village of Kaniów (Kanev), only a few miles downstream from Kiev. He had come too early. The Russian court remained in Kiev awaiting the coming of Spring before setting out on the river. Life in Kaniów was dull. Living conditions were primitive and there were few amusements.(48)

Potemkin and Bezborodko headed the stream of visitors from Kiev who gave some respite to the monotony. Potemkin, the leading spirit in Russia's plans to expand south, abandoned his support of the Polish Opposition in order to court Stanisław August. Nominally a Polish citizen through purchase of an estate in southeastern Poland, Potemkin came dressed in Polish costume and wore his Polish St. Stanisław medal.(49) As an expression of his friendship towards the Polish king, Potemkin contributed 100,000 rubles towards the expenses of the king's journey.(50) The two met several times with Stackelberg, Bezborodko, and the Prince of Nassau. Stanisław August complained about Branicki's opposition politics and presented his plan for a Russo-Polish alliance supported by a strong, reformed Poland. Bezborodko, like Potemkin, encouraged the Polish king, but warned him that the necessary war with Turkey would not come immediately.(51)

The Russian empress had left Tsarskoe Selo, her palace outside Petersburg, in mid-January 1787. She spent a month travelling to Kiev where Potemkin had arranged such a reception that the Prince de Ligne thought "Louis XIV would have turned green with envy or would have married Catherine to get such a spectacular reception."(52) Many distinguished foreigners accepted invitations to accompany her. The ambassadors of France, England, Austria, and Poland came as did two of the most brilliant courtiers of the day, the Prince de Ligne and the Prince of Nassau. Numerous Poles gathered in Kiev to pay homage to the Russian empress. The heads of the Opposition appeared: Branicki with his Russian wife, Ignacy and Szczęsny Potocki, Kazimierz Sapieha, and Seweryn Rzewuski. Royalists also established quarters in Kiev where they were joined by visitors from Kaniów: Stanislaw and Józef Poniatowski, Michał Mniszech, Ludwik Tyszkiewicz, Kazimierz Plater, and Bishop Naruszewicz.(53)

Members of the Opposition quickly opened political conversations at

Kiev designed to capture the empress's favor. Branicki suggested, as in 1776, replacing Stackelberg with Alexander Engelhardt, Branicki's brother-in-law. Others discussed the possibility of making one of the Russian empress's grandchildren king of Poland when the throne became vacant, thus betraying their lack of commitment to that fundamental Polish liberty, elective monarchy. Curiously, Maurice Glaire had proposed the same idea to Stanisław August.(54)

Not even their former supporter, Prince Potemkin, paid any attention to the Opposition's arguments.Potemkin advised Branicki to seek reconciliation with Stanisław August and tried to arrange a meeting between the two.(55) Igancy Potocki found himself excluded from the empress's table and frequently from her presence altogether.(56) Even Branicki absented himself from public gatherings on the pretext of illness while Kazimierz Sapieha's loud conversation brought public rebuke from a Russian who told him that Kiev was "neither Warsaw nor a diet."(57) Catherine granted a friendly welcome only to Szczęsny Potocki whom she hoped could be won over by flattery.(58)

Despite the Russians' hostility to leaders of the Polish Opposition, Catherine made it clear that she would not give Stanisław August a completely free hand in ruling Poland. While Catherine granted Bishop Naruszewicz a jeweled cross and a pension and presented Mniszech's wife with the St. Catherine medal, she also awarded that medal to Branicki's wife.(59) Indeed, the Russian empress could be seen to observe "a perfect balance between the two contending parties neither encouraging one, or showing any dissatisfaction with the other."(60)

After waiting for more than a month for the Dniepr to become navigable, the Russians made ready to move. The ships anchored opposite Kaniów on May 6 and Bezborodko came ashore to Stanislaw August aboard together with Stanisław Poniatowski, Ludwik Tyskiewicz, Bishop Naruszewicz, Antoni Deboli, and General Komarzewski. The Russians also invited the British and French envoys, Charles Whitworth and Joseph de Maisonneuve. After a forty-five minute trip in the rain through the Dniepr sandbars, the party reached the Russian fleet where they were greeted with music and cannon salutes.(61)

The courtly world eagerly awaited the first meeting of two sovereigns who had been lovers thirty years before. When the Polish king mounted the deck, he found himself surrounded by courtiers, anxious to see "the first emotions and to hear the first words of the august persons in a situation so different from that in which they had seen each other before." To the sentimental world of the late eighteenth century, Catherine and Stanisław were "united by love, separated by jealousy, and pursued by hatred."(62) Nevertheless, the principals displayed no obvious emotion although some observers professed to see the Russian empress "a little troubled." Stanisław August was distressed to find himself received with the stiff ceremony of full royal honors. He had hoped to come as "Count Poniatowski" to save precious time for negotiations. Catherine called him "a king and her friend." She decreed that the day would be devoted entirely to festivities.(63)

Stanisław August and Potemkin returned to the empress's galley for setting out what he hoped to receive from Russia. Abandoning for the moment all attempts at constitutional reform, the king requested a formal alliance which would protect Poland from future partition and assure Russia of a monopoly of influence. The king asked for exclusive rights to grant patronage in Poland but pledged to advance only those persons whom Russia recommended. For the alliance, he offered Russia 25,000 - 30,000 soldiers in time of war (to be raised and equipped at Russian expense) if that power would permit Poland to increase her troop strength from 24,000 to 36,000 men.(64) Since Russia had been on the brink of war with Turkey in 1777 and 1783, Stanisław August hoped that Catherine's tour of Crimea signified a situation favorable to Polish involvement.

Stanisław August dined with the Empress and Potemkin on board the Russian galley. After dinner, Potemkin took the king to his ship where Branicki waited and tried unsuccessfully to force an apology from him. (Potemkin later told Stanisław August that evil counsel from Ignacy Potocki and Adam Czartoryski were responsible for Branicki's obstinacy; Potemkin promised to keep working on Branicki.)(65) The most important meeting came with Catherine's secretary Bezborodko, who promised to prevent unpleasantness at the 1788 diet by means of a confederation. Stackelberg, also present, assured Stanisław August that the idea of an alliance would definitely please Catherine. Bezborodko, nevertheless, dashed the king's hopes for immediate action claiming that the German powers would not permit an extraordinary diet to be summoned in Poland to ratify an alliance.(66)

Stanisław August and Potemkin returned to the empress's gallery for final leavetaking. Catherine once again avoided political discussion and spoke only in personal terms. Finally, she made her farewells, pleading fatigue. As the Polish king left the imperial galley, Catherine remarked, "Oh! how he has changed — he must say the same about me."(67) Potemkin complained bitterly that he had been compromised because the empress had not given the king more time. Stackelberg and the Prince of Nassau tried to make up for the abrupt dismissal by assuring Stanisław that he had won Potemkin's complete favor.(68) Stanisław August gave a festive dinner that evening which many Russians attended. After dinner, magnificent fireworks lit up the countryside.(69)

The Russian fleet departed early the following morning, but Stanisław August soon met another crowned head, Joseph II, who was on his way to meet Catherine. Stanisław August sent his nephew, Stanisław Poniatowski, to the emperor's camp to arrange a meeting but Joseph himself came immediately.(70) Behaving in a friendly manner, Joseph gave his imperial word of honor that he would not only refrain from "taking from Poland a single inch of ground or a single tree" but that he would prevent anyone else from partitioning Poland. The emperor specifically instructed Stanisław August to cite his words publicly.(71)

The Prince de Ligne remarked maliciously later that Stanisław August "spent three months and three million Polish zlotys to see the empress for three hours."(72) While this statement is literally close to the truth, the Polish king had reason to feel satisfied. Eighteenth-century diplomacy centered on personalities and "summit meetings" significantly affected political developments. The king's politeness touched Catherine who became "resolved to protect him against the attacks of his enemies." More significantly, Stanislaw August removed an old emnity at the Russian court through reconciliation with Potemkin who promised to restrict Branicki's freedom to attack the king. Both Potemkin and Bezborodko took the king's offer of an alliance seriously. In addition, Stanisław August's success with Joseph II seemed to remove the underpinnings of the Austrian party and the intrigues of Austrian envoys in Warsaw. Concretely, Stanisław August emerged from the meeting at Kaniów with approval of his plans for a confederated diet, which he had sought every since 1777, and hope of alliance with Russia. Needless to say, Stanisław August owed this success to more than sentiment. Russia and Austria were about to embark on a war against Turkey. Supporting the Polish king promised to prevent the kind of disturbance which would distract the partners' attention from partition of the Ottoman Empire.

Shortly after his return to Warsaw, Stanisław August sent Catherine a draft proposal of a treaty of alliance. The king wanted Poland to join actively in the war against Turkey with an expeditionary corps of 20,000 troops in exchange for minor expeditionary corps of 20,000 troops in exchange for minor constitutional reforms, monetary subsidies from Russia to enlarge the Polish army, and substantial territorial concessions in Bessarabia and Moldavia.(73) The alliance was to be enacted by an extraordinary diet which would meet as a confederation formed in the Permanent Council, as in 1776. This time, however, the confederation would come into existence even before the dietines thus making them confederated. Stackelberg stood entirely behind the king's plans.(74)

Catherine received the Polish proposal without great enthusiasm. She agreed in principle to an alliance in order to keep the king's enemies from trying to topple the Polish government during Russia's preoccupation with Turkey. Nevertheless, she categorically refused to take immediate action.(75) The empress also rejected offers from Opposition members Franciszek Branicki, Seweryn Rzewuski, and Szczęsny Potocki, to organize local confederations, which would eventually unite into a national confederation, and mobilize troops to share in the war with Turkey. Thus, the Opposition aimed once again at replacing Stanisław August and Stackelberg as Catherine's most important instruments in Poland. They succeeded in winning Potemkin away from his brief friendship with the Polish king with their proposals. The Russian was searching eagerly for any source of military aid during the difficult first months of the military campaign against Turkey which began in August 1787.(76)

Russia formally replied to Stanisław August's request for an alliance in June 1788, nine months after the Polish king had made his proposals. While Catherine endorsed the alliance, her terms were distinctly unfavorable to Poland. She would permit no constitutional reforms, whatsoever, nor any territorial expansion. Furthermore, Catherine reduced the proposed number of Polish troops to 12,000 which would consist of three 4,000 man brigades under the command of Prince Stanisław Poniatowski and two members of the Opposition, Franciszek Branicki and Szczęsny Potocki. What is more, the Russian armies of Potemkin and Rumiantsev would divide the Polish troops. Even worse, Catherine offered to pay Poland for her troops in six yearly installments beginning after the conclusion of peace with Turkey. Slight modifications made through negotiation would not make the Russian plan more palatable to the king. Nevertheless, Stanisław August decided to conclude the alliance to avoid offending the empress and, perhaps, to gain concessions for himself personally, if not for the country.(77)

The dietines for the 1788 diet took place in August amid great tension. Encouraged by their effect at the 1786 diet, magnates put forward their maximum effort in their home districts. Thousands of nobles recruited by Adam Czartoryski, Stanisław Potocki, and other

Opposition leaders, attended the Lublin dietine and elected all six deputies from their camp. Similar massive efforts gave the Opposition about 40% of the deputies to the diet, a substantially higher percent than they had ever won before. Stanisław August expressed dismay at the success of Opposition propaganda with its accent on hostility to the Permanent Council. Nevertheless, his forces still held a majority.(78)

The 1788 diet opened, as usual, in October but developed in such a way as to change the course of Polish history. As planned by King Stanisław August and Russian ambassador Stackelberg, the diet quickly formed a confederation to enlarge the army and gather new taxes so as to form a military alliance with Russia. The unexpected occurred, however, in the sudden diplomatic intervention of Prussia, which dramatically broke with her co-partitioners.(79)

Frederick William II, successor to the Prussian throne after 'the death of his uncle, Frederick the Great, in 1786, resolved to initiate a new course in foreign policy. Prussian diplomats viewed the Russo-Turkish war as a marvellous opportunity to gain terrority in Poland. Count Ewald Hertzberg proposed a fanciful exchange plan according to which Russia's and Austria's conquests in the Balkans would be balanced by Poland's cession to Prussia of the lower Vistula region including Gdańsk, while Poland would be compensated with recovery of Austrian Galicia. Austrian chancellor Kaunitz refused the plan so that Prussia would not gain from Austrian feats of arms and convinced Russia to issue a joint guarantee of Polish territorial integrity. Prussia, therefore, came to consider any Polish-Russian alliance inimical to her interests and instructed Buchholtz in Warsaw to block the conclusion of the treaty at the diet.(80)

Buchholtz's ensuing intervention caused a storm which jolted the diet off the tracks laid down by the king and Russian ambassador. At the first full session, the Prussian formally protested against the conclusion of a Russo-Polish treaty and held out to Poland the possibility of alliance with Prussia. Flattered at being courted by a major power and carried away by the possibility of independent action, the Polish diet responded by authorizing an increase in the army to 100,000 without, however, enacting any new taxes to pay for it. Prussia misinterpreted this as a move towards military alliance with Russia and quickly dispatched a more experienced diplomat, the Italian Girilomo Lucchesini, to take over in Warsaw. Lucchesini carried instructions to play the role of *agent provocateur,* to build a pro-Prussian party which would inflame traditional anti-Russian sentiment at the diet until Russia intervened openly. Prussia would then send an expeditionary corps at the request of the pro-Prussian Poles, but instead of fighting the Russians, they would seize Gdańsk and other north Poland territories. Prussia felt secure in this bold attack on Russian primacy in Poland because Russia was deeply engaged in a war against Turkey and against Sweden, which had opened up a second front in order to regain Baltic territories.(81)

The bold Prussian initiative met encouraging response within Poland. As a result of their failure to win over Catherine II at Kiev in 1787, a group of Polish Opposition leaders turned to Berlin for support. Prince Adam Czartoryski, seconded by the Lithuanian Marshal of the Confederated Diet Kazimierz Nestor Sapieha, Ignacy Potocki, Michał Ogiński, and Karol Radziwiłł worked together at the 1788 diet to gather a majority of the deputies. With the aid of the Prussian envoys, especially Lucchesini, who was unusually captivating, the Opposition succeeded in convincing numerous royalists to abandon the king. An unbridled enthusiasm gripped the deputies as the Opposition fanned the flames of anti-Russian feeling. Fearing that this "too-strong horse" would run away, Stanisław August appealed to Stackelberg to end the confederation as soon as possible.(82)

Before any action was taken, the Opposition used their majority to dismantle the system which had governed Poland since 1775. Disregarding Russia's voluntary withdrawal of her offer of alliance and Stackelberg's warning that the Empress would cease to regard Poland as a friendly nation if she violated the guarantee of 1775, the diet moved to make Poland fully independent. The Opposition convinced most deputies in a 16-hour session that the Permanent Council was a foreign institution imposed on them by Russia and forced a vote by secret ballot which abolished the Military Department. Control over the army fell to the Military Commissions established in 1764 which were dominated by the hetmen. The diet also demanded full withdrawal of Russian troops stationed in southeastern Poland to guard Russian communications with the Turkish front. Enraged, Stackelberge asked that Stanisław August break with the confederation and use Russian armies to conquer his country (just as Prussia had hoped he would) but the king wished to avoid the kind of isolation he had suffered during the war of the Bar Confederation and made concessions to the diet. With the prolongation of the diet beyond its normal six-week term, the Foreign Affairs Department of the Permanent Council was abolished in favor of a parliamentary committee and, one month later in January 1789, the Permanent Council itself was ended.(83)

In fifteen short weeks from the opening of the diet on October 6 until January 19, 1789, the Opposition succeeded in realizing traditional

Polish republican dreams,. At long last, the diet had stripped the king of his constitutional power over the army, foreign affairs, and internal administration. Russia, the protector of the Permanent Council, was expelled from Poland. The future would see whether the Opposition would succeed in modernizing Poland more effectively than the system it replaced.

CHAPTER VI

EPILOGUE: REFORM AND PARTITION

Having seized control of the government, the Opposition did not know what to do. The major impulse of the diet had been patriotic, but negative. The newly-dominant faction called itself the Patriotic Party and aimed to restore full independence through the rejection of foreign control, chiefly by challenging Russia. The upsurge of national feeling led deputies to make intemperate speeches attacking and even ridiculing the formerly all-powerful Russian ambassador. They offered no solution to the pressing military, political, economic, social, and cultural problems which had created Poland's weakness in relation to her neighbors. Indeed, the patriotic movement represented, in the short run, a step backwards. The Permanent Council provided an orderly form of administration and could prepare legislation for submission to the diet. The institution could have been captured and used by the "Patriots" to launch their reforms, but instead they dismantled it and lugubriously drafted a new constitution.

The triumph of the Patriotic Party was accompanied by Sarmatian fantasies. Prominent members of the Opposition ostentatiously discarded their French jackets in favor of Polish caftans in order to whip up enthusiasm among their supporters. A popular verse of the day proclaimed that "as long as Poles were not ashamed of their dress, the country was whole. The Poles were well off then. Long coats and long boundaries. Today Poles in short jackets have short boundaries."(1)

The vices of traditional Polish parliamentarianism returned too. There was no agenda. Speakers raised any matter they chose regardless of the issue on the floor. Deptuies moved around at will, interrupting, discussing, quarrelling, and occasionally fighting with each other. Rational discussion of business was difficult. One parliamentarian complained after a year that "what we could have done in fourteen weeks has taken us fourteen months. Much has been abolished but nothing takes its place". Austrian minister de Caché reported that "parliamentary gatherings increasingly make an impression of chaos" as the king and ministers were pushed aside by "genry democracy" (*demokracja szlachecka*).(2)

The most important issue facing the diet was how to maintain Poland's new independence. One was through building a strong army. In October 1788, the newly-convened diet moved amidst great enthusiasm to raise an army of 100,000 soldiers, more than five times the number presently under arms. Since the country was hopelessly unprepared to finance this and since the traditional Polish gentry considered itself a warrior elite, the diet decided in February 1789 to fill the army with "national cavalry", composed largely of untrained, ill-disciplined nobles. The decision was political. Maintenance of the lesser gentry by the magnates had long been a basic feature of the Sarmatian politics and, in recent years, the Opposition had worked against the king's efforts to professionalize the army. Hetman Branicki, who expected to benefit from the situation was particularly vociferous on that point. Only Prince Stanisław Poniatowski, the king's nephew, dared remind the diet of what everyone with military experience knew, namely, that the well-drilled, well-equipped infantry of Europe's regular armies could brush aside Poland's national cavalry without difficulty. He was denounced so harshly in the diet and in the streets that he left the country never to return. The diet was later to reverse itself and move towards greater professionalization.

The more sober leaders of the Patriotic Party considered that Poland could not protect herself without a powerful ally. When Prussia offered herself, the Patriots jumped. Their leaders had come to favor a Prussian orientation even before the opening of the diet but the signing of the alliance among Prussia, Great Britain, and Holland made an anti-Russian military campaign appear imminent. With Prussian intervention at the diet, the Patriots requested that formal ties be established. The scheme had some merit, especially in 1788 and 1789, but most Poles considered only the advantages to their country and were not willing to pay the price of Prussian support: Gdańsk, Torun, and the Pomeranian Coast. A defensive treaty was signed in March 1790 based on the unspoken exchange agreement which would give Prussia these areas when Galicia was restored to Poland after war with Austria. When the Polish diet refused to consider the alienation of Polish territory, the treaty evaporated leaving behind only a scrap of paper.

These real problems of governing Poland and maintaining her independence precipitated the dissolution of the Patriotic Party. Taxation may have been the final straw. After abolishing the Permanent Council, the diet had no machinery to collect taxes. An appeal for voluntary contributions met little response and the diet resorted to contracting large foreign loans. The more responsible members of the party, like

Ignacy Potocki, Adam Czartoryski, Stanisław Malachowski, and the Old Bar Confederate, Bishop Adam Krasiński, who made his first appearance at the diet in twenty years, understood that the nobility must take on financial responsibilities. In March 1789, the diet approved a tax of 10 % of regular annual income for nobles and 20 % for clergy; many Church lands were also nationalized. The administrative machinery, unfortunately, was not equal to the task of collecting the money. No method of checking income had been devised. Nobles and clergy swore to its size before specially appointed commissioners. Some nobles paid conscientiously but many did not. Perhaps one-third of the sum that should have been collected actually found its way to the treasury.(3)

Seeing that the diet was not living up to its potential, Hugo Kołłątaj published a pamphlet late in 1790 which sought to distinguish between "true" and "false" patriots, instead of thinking in terms of a united party. The "false" patriots, in Kołłątaj's view, were those who were merely republicans and patriots without a vision of what was needed to build up the strength of the Polish state. The "true" patriots agreed with the "false" ones that the Permanent Council was an alien institution that had to be abolished and that the alliance of Russia should be dropped, but they went further. They wished to create a new government and pass whatever reforms were needed to increase national strength. Alliance with Prussia was required for Poland to achieve freedom from Russia.

The measures that were initiated in 1789 bore fruit in 1790 and 1791. Bills came out of committees (called "delegations") and new procedural rules allowed the diet to deal with them efficiently. An important law limited participation in dietines to land-holding and tax paying nobles. This seemingly undemocratic measure excluded about 400,000 nobles from political rights but it actually made the dietines operate in a more democratic manner since it effectively restricted the power of the great magnates by depriving them of the services of their retainers. Governing Commissions (*komisje porządkowe cywilno-woyskowe*) were created in the various provinces to administer military matters (like recruitment, quartering, and supply) as well as economic matters (like tax collection, fire control, parish schooling, poor relief, and control of vagabonds). Elected at the dietines by the local nobles, the commissions initiated no social change. However, they provided an alternative system of government to the centralized machinery of absolutist Europe. As the army grew in size, it was more closely regulated. The officer corps was given additional training and some manoeuvres were held.

The cities received sympathetic attention. In November 1789, the urban government of Warsaw, stimulated and assisted by Kołłątaj, gathered support from 140 other towns and cities to process solemnly to the Royal Castle and present to the king their requests for fuller self-governing rights and representation in the diet. Only the medieval capital, Kraków, refused to join the common action; it sent a separate delegation with its own program. Many members of the diet were outraged at what seemed an imitation of revolutionary France, but by April 18, 1791, enough support had been gathered to permit passage of a substantial reform bill. Property-owning burghers were given the right to judicial due process and permitted to purchase landed estates or gain appointment to civil and military office. Automatic nobilitation was granted to burghers who purchased an entire village or town. Immediately after the law passed on April 18, 1791 about two hundred burghers were ennobled.

The economic, social, and military reforms were accompanied by a new look at the constitution, the diet chose a committee in September 1789 to draw up plans "to improve the form of Government". Ignacy Potocki headed the committee which also included royalists and "false" patriots. In December, the committee presented a document to the diet which prepared a set of republican principles instead of the draft constitution originally intended. Despite radical-looking phrases about "citizens" and the "Nation", political rights were restricted to the nobility. The elected kingship was also reaffirmed but the king was to lose most of his powers of appointment and the senate was also to decline to largely ceremonial powers. Virtually full legislative and executive authority was to rest in the lower chamber which would become more efficient thanks to limitations on the *liberum veto*, which would remain in full force only for constitutional issues. Unanimous consent of provincial dietines was also required for major changes. Potocki was the principal author but his ideas were not as radically republican as the final document.

Potocki found his preparation of the "principles" a grueling experience. The effort of drafting and passing his first piece of legislation left him discouraged and exhausted. Every step had to be argued and manoeuvered through the undisciplined, talkative deputies. He dreamed of finishing "this unhappy constitution" and going to Italy. His ideas began to change. Potocki decided that "Poland is not made for freedom . . . For a certain time, royalist government will be most appropriate."(4)

Years of political enmity made it extremely difficult for Potocki and

Poniatowski to achieve reconciliation, but in May 1790, Potocki asked the king for his ideas on constitutional reform in writing and promised to give his own. For further consultations, the face-saving expedient was adopted of working through an intermediary to conduct discussions. Scipio Piattoli, an Italian priest who had been employed by Potocki's mother-in-law, Princess Elżbieta Lubomirska, but who had recently entered the king's service, was chosen. From May 1790 until the enactment of the constituion one year later Piattoli met with both men and expertly assisted them to the compromise which they both wished to reach.

King Stanisław August had long dreamed of far-reaching political reform, but bitter experience had made him cautious. He finally presented to Piattoli his reform proposals which aimed at a constitutional monarchy with an hereditary throne which he hoped would pass to one of his nephews. The king would have the power of nomination and appointment traditionally held by elective kings. Executive authority would be exercized by a cabinet composed of ministers chosen by the diet but appointed by the king. They would serve only for a limited period. Thus, a king who achieved political supremacy thanks to his patronage powers, would be able to dominate public affairs.

A compromise project was worked out with the assistance of other persons, most notably Hugo Kołłątaj, the former rector of the Jagiellonian University. Kołłątaj had come to Warsaw in 1787 and distinguished himself as a publicist and organizer of ''The Forge'', a group of reformist publicists. Kołłątaj's *Anonymous Letters to Stanisław Malachowski,* the Marshal of the Diet, were published in 1788-89 while another book, *The Political Law of the Polish Nation* appeared in 1790. Kołłątaj favored a strictly republican constitution with a governing diet and a figurehead king, but he had good connection with the royal family and was willing to compromise on political matters in order to move on to a general consideration of social and economic reform. Kołłątaj hoped to bring the upper bourgeoisie into the political nation and develop a modern commercial and manufacturing system in Poland through the passage of an ''economic constitution'' revising serfdom and creating a national bank.

While the king and the leaders of the ''true'' patriots achieved compromise among themselves, they feared that they could not pass the resulting legislation through the diet. The provincial elections of November 1790 showed that no appeal could be made to the provinces which remained staunchly conservative. Fifty of fifty-five dietines declared themselves in principle against an hereditary throne (but permitted, as an exception, the election of the elector of Saxony during the life-time of Stanisław August). Many also sent instructions requesting the diet not to interfere with traditional liberties, not to grant the burghers additional rights, and not to interfere with the national cavalry.(5) Since two years had elapsed after the start of the diet, a second slate of deputies was also elected. A novel method was adopted, however, of having them join the old deputies at work thereby doubling the size of the diet. This permitted the work to continue. Starting a new diet would have required winding up the confederation, which had made the work of the diet possible, and starting a new one, a measure which might have resulted in foreign intervention. Once in Warsaw, the new deputies fell under the influence of the leaders of the diet.

The reformist group decided to organize a *coup d'état* in order to change the constitution. While most deputies were home for Easter holidays, a secret call sent out for reformists to return to Warsaw. On May 3, 1791, the Royal Castle, where the diet met, was surrounded by army detachments supplied by Prince Józef Poniatowski while crowds of burghers organized by the guilds gathered in the streets. The galleries of the diet were packed with supporters of the changes. The events of the day had been worked out in advance, beginning from reports from Polish diplomats abroad about the dangers of Poland's current position, to the swearing allegiance to the new constitution. Some room was left for improvization, however. Opponents spoke and acted freely. Had more been present, the new legislation might have been shouted down. Only clear numerical inferiority kept opponents from drawing their sabres. The legislation was read only once and no formal vote was taken, contrary to normal procedures. 282 of the 500 deputies and senators were present, about the average number for an ordinary session. 110 favored the legislation while 72 opposed.

In the area of "fundamental law", the May 3 constitution at long last abolished the *liberum veto* so that effective parliamentary debate could take place. It also eliminated another major problem of Polish parliamentary practice by providing that the diet would be subject to call at any time within its two-year mandate. It would receive instructions from the provincial dietines but would not be bound by them. The Polish throne became hereditary but lost independent sources of power. As the commissions of 1764 were merged with the Permanent Council of 1775 in a more manageable form, executive authority came to rest in the hands of a cabinet composed of the king, as presiding officer, the Primate of the Church, and five ministers, who headed five "commissions'': police, chancellory, foreign affairs, war, and treasury. Selection of the members of the new cabinet, or "Guard of Laws" as it was called, was made from the traditional corps of ministers. Appointments came from the king, but a 2/3 vote of no-confidence would remove a minister from the cabinet. Stanisław August successfully used his political skills to dominate the diet and the cabinet during the one year in which the May 3 constitution existed. His successors would probably have been less successful.

Social measures formed part of the May 3 act. The chief beneficiaries were the burghers of the royal cities whose gains of April 18 were reaffirmed. In addition, the burghers achieved limited political rights within the national forum. They could now send twenty-four non-voting "plenipotentiaries" to the diet. The peasants gained far less. Keeping in mind the fate of the Zamoyski Law Code of 1780 which failed to pass the diet in large part because of provisions in favor of the peasants, the authors of the May 3 constitution only put the peasantry under national "protection". Landlords were encouraged but not required to put peasant obligations in written form so that the courts could supervise their fulfillment.

The May 3 constitution was a progressive document which broke the procedural logjam holding reform up for decades. It signaled the end of partisan political warfare between royalist and republican advocates of reform. The way was cleared for approval of a large backlog of measures which had accumulated over a long time. The diet efficiently drew up and passed legislation setting up the governmental institutions created by the May 3 constitution, although it embued them with a more republican, and less centralized, flavor than the constitution had implied.(6) Reformers like Hugo Kołłątaj saw the May document as a "political" constitution which would quickly be supplemented by "economic" and "moral" constitutions. While it seems unlikely that Polish society had changed enough to permit major peasant reform, it is probable that many new measures would have passed improving trade, industry, and banking. A serious obstacle to progress in this area remained in the unwillingness of the Polish cities and their supporters to grant equal rights to Jews, who equalled the Polish burghers in number and wealth.

The proponents of the new constitution did not leave its reception in the provinces to chance. They used all their political strength to augment genuine support in order to give the impression of unanimous national jubiliation. The king distributed orders, medals, and jobs in the provinces. Both he and the "true" patriots instructed their supporters throughout the country to organize public expressions of thanks. Most of the provincial governing commissions passed such resolutions. Constitutionalists dominating these and other bodies refused to register all protests.(7)

Active support sprang up within Warsaw. An "Assembly of Friends of the Constitution" was founded by a number of deputies and their supporters from outside the diet. The assembly acted like a modern political party (or a club in revolutionary France), binding its members to support decisions taken by majority vote at sessions held in advance of the actual meetings of the diet. Membership in the club included royalists, republicans, socially-minded educators, several burghers, and, of course, some opportunists.

Nevertheless, the provisions of the May 3 act and the method of its passage aroused much dissatisfaction. A group of deputies tried to present official protests to the king and the government of the city of Warsaw, but their protests were refused. Gaining no satisfaction here, most deputies sought allies in the provinces. Large sections of the country, notably Lithuania, Wołyń, and the Lublin and Sandomierz districts wrote official protests which, once again, were refused. Some pamphlets attacking the new laws appeared.

Hearing the news from Poland, Szczęsny Potocki and Seweryn Rzewuski, the chief opponents of constitutional reform, who had left the country earlier in disgust, decided to overthrow the new regime. They thought that a royal dictatorship had been created. In traditional Polish style, they had strong ideas about how Poland should be governed and the financial means to act. Potocki favored creation of a federal republic composed of three provinces, each with its own government. He hoped to produce a more virtuous, and therefore better, government. A king would act as the figurehead for a ceremonial central government. Rzewuski's ideas ran differently. A violent anti-royalist who supported the French and American Revolutions (doubtless failing to understand their social significance), he sought to abolish the monarchy altogether or, at the very least, to return full executive authority to the ministers, as it had been before the reforms of the 1760's.

Failing to convince the Austrian court to support them, both men went to the headquarters of the Russian army at Jassy and conspired with Potemkin and Bezborodko. A few corrupt politicans and adventure joined them, most notably Franciszek Branicki. But idealist or cynic, the calculation was perfectly sound in foreign policy terms. Prussia could not be counted on as an ally because she herself had designs on Polish territory while Austria was too involved with Revolutionary France to pay much attention. Only Russia could protect Polish territorial integrity.

But would she? By 1792, Russia had given up on Poland. The patriotic deputies had cast too many insults at Russia, had unilaterally renounced Russia's guarantee of Polish territorial integrity and had refused to let her supply her armies through Polish territory during the war against Turkey. Foreign policy entered in the decision, too. Catherine was violently opposed to the French revolution and allowed partition in order to turn Prussia against France. When the Turkish War ended with the Treaty of Jassy in January 1792, Russian troops were free to turn against Poland. As a pretext, Russia gathered the Polish malcontents and had them form a confederation. The "Targowica" Confederation was signed in St. Petersburg on 24 April 1792. Russian armies entered Poland in May.

Faced with Russian invasion, few leaders of the constitutional movement tried to defend their work. Military action was fought as a delaying tactic while political negotiations were carried out between the Polish king and Jakub Bulgakov, who had succeeded Stackelberg as Russian ambassador. At his demand, Poniatowski acceded to Targowica, which he hoped to capture from within. Kołłątaj tried to imitate him but was refused. Ignacy Potocki and others chose exile, chiefly in Saxony, rather than take part in the new system but they kept in close and sympathetic touch with their Warsaw colleagues, hoping the king would rescue some part of what the Four Year Diet had accomplished and permit them to come home. Their hopes ebbed, however, as Targowica proved instransigeant. The confederates annulled the work of the confederated diet and applied strict press censorship. Russia required that Polish armies be disarmed.

Russian plans to partition Poland for a second time leaked out. While groups in exile conspired actively for an armed uprising, public dissatisfaction with Targowica grew rapidly, fueled also by unemployment caused by the collapse of the major Warsaw banks. When General Antoni Madaliński refused orders in March 1794 for his troops to lay down their arms, insurrection broke out. Uprisings followed in the Kraków district, which invited General Tadeusz Kościuszko to come as representative of the exiles, and later in the cities of Warsaw and Wilno. As local uprisings spread, Russia (and Prussia, when she sent in her troops) had to withdraw in order to fight a full military action. This gave the Poles a chance to organize a provisional government.

The new government was caught between two fires when it came to reform. Most participants supported the May 3 constitution and wanted no further change. The Kraków group even made Kościuszko swear to introduce no new legislation before summoning a regular diet. A man of his word, Kościuszko tried to maintain the principle. He accepted appointment as "dictator" and head of the provisional government only for the duration of the emergency.

This plan was not entirely satisfactory, however. The uprising in Warsaw on April 17, 1794, when the Warsaw population, organized by guild groups, expelled the Russian garrison from the city without assistance from regular Polish troops, showed that non-nobles could add much to the success of the uprising. A group of idealistic lesser nobles and clerics, precursors of the nineteenth century intelligentsia, who were inspired by the ideals of the French Revolution, formed a "Jacobin" Club, carried on a public propaganda campaign, and tried to pressure the government into social reform. Their main efforts, however, went into convincing the government to prosecute the war as strongly as possible. The "Jacobins" were the organizers of the events of May and June 1794 when Targowica dignitaries were taken from prison and hanged in order to raise public morale and dig a gulf between the Uprising and the Old Regime. While not implicated in the affair, Hugo Kołłątaj became more and more favorable to the Jacobins as time went on.

Mass action alienated the still conservative Polish gentry. Kościuszko harshly repressed the Warsaw insurgents arresting more than 1,000 participants. A number of the richer residents left the capital for their country estates, which were already, or soon would be, under occupation. They made their separate peace with Russia and Prussia. Still, enough support was found to permit the Polanice Decree which freed the peasants from feudal obligations for the length of their service in the insurrectionary army, restricted the work-dues of all peasants slightly, and granted them their personal freedom. These measures convinced several thousand peasants to join Kościuszko's armies. Detachments of scythemen decided the battle of Racławice in his favor.

The Poles had no real hope against their numerous, well-armed and well-trained opponents, however valiantly they fought. Kościuszko was wounded and captured at Maciejowice. The Russian army headed by General Aleksandr Suvorov laid siege to the Praga suburb of Warsaw. After storming it, he cold-bloodedly massacred several thousand men, women, and children. Many of the victims were Jews.

Across the river, Warsaw understood and surrendered. The insurrectionary armies laid down their arms shortly thereafter. Russia,

Prussia, and Austria carried out a third partition which the Diet of Grodno was forced to ratify. King Stanisław August Poniatowski abdicated on October 25, 1795 ending the last vestiges of Polish statehood.

CHAPTER VII

CONCLUSIONS

In *The Second Partition of Poland*, R.H. Lord remarked that if Poland had disappeared in 1772 as a result of the first partition "the world would have said that the Poles deserved their fate" because Poland was "at the moment of her deepest degredation". Twenty years later, however, at the time of the second partition, Poland "was beginning to put forth new life and to show her greatest patriotism and energy". The sudden eruption of the Four Year Diet, the Constitution of May 3, and the Kościuszko Uprising provided "tragic but ennobling experiences" which kept pride and nationalism alive throughout the nineteenth century.(1) Subsequent research has shown the standing of national reform to be somewhat better in the 1760's and not quite as glorious in the 1780's and 1790's, as Lord thought. But there can be no doubt that much had changed in those years.

After the first partition, the spread of Enlightenment culture accelerated. New magazines brought philosophical and literary works to the public and Polish literary talents developed rapidly. King Stanisław August carried on his cultural politics in Warsaw, which became the leading center for artistic expression. Other nobles, especially Prince Adam Czartoryski, formed similar artistic centers on their estates near Warsaw and in the provinces. Reform brought the younger generation entirely under the influence of the Enlightenment. Private schools like the Royal Cadet School provided a good secular education while promoting a spirit of patriotism and public service. The National Education Commission saved schooling from collapse after the dissolution of the Jesuit Order in 1773 and continued the work of modernization.

Progress in other areas was not as rapid as in literature, the arts, and education. The Polish economy changed little. Cultivation of grain for export predominated but the years of peace after the first partition revived production. Some new signs appeared, particularly with the replacement of labor-dues by monetary rent on some estates and the consequent spread of the monied economy. Manufacturing and com-

merce grew although not on a firm basis. Poland also made some
progress in providing orderly administrative machinery. The Permanent
Council, the chief distinguishing feature of the period 1775-88, offered
on paper an effieicnt system compatible with eighteenth century
standards. Political problems, however, prevented the Council from
fulfilling its promise. Good work was accomplished, however, by the
Commissions of Good Order. (under the Police Department), the
Crown Treasury Commission (under the Treasury Department), and
the Military Department.

These changes in culture, education, economics, and administration
put Poland in position to emerge from its status as the ''sick man'' of
eighteenth century Europe, but the political process made that very
difficult to accomplish. Despite the first partition, there was little sense
of impending doom and little realization that old prejudices should be
put aside to forestall further partition. As the ancient rivalry between
royalists and republicans continued unabated, Poland presented almost
as weak a face to the world in 1788 as she had in 1775.

Stanisław August Poniatowski aimed at being king in fact as well as in
name. Despite constitutional weakness, he succeeded in retaining
political supremacy by subordinating himself to Russian demands.
Through Russia, Poniatowski gained support for his Royal Party which
generally dominated diets and dietines. The first decade of his reign
taught the king the dangers of isolation and he resigned himself to
Russian domination. He continued to hope that some day Russia would
permit thorough constitutional overhaul.

Poniatowski well understood the need to transform Polish institutions
and educate the public. He spared no energy in promoting the spread of
the Enlightenment and the growth of the economy. A political being as
well as a cultural one, Stanisław August advanced many measures to
strengthen his own position but he had no plans to create royal ab-
solutism. The king followed a policy of national unity that offered high
position within his system to nobles (including former opponents) who
would support him and his program, which consisted of reform
measures acceptable to Russia.

Russia controlled Poland from 1775 to 1788 and set the limits of
reform. Catherine II had not really desired the first partition and Russian
policy aimed at securing all that remained. Nikita Panin, head of the
College of Foreign Affairs, wanted to maintain the *status quo* in Europe
in cooperation with Prussia. In order to keep Poland peaceful, he
supported a stronger centralized system of government (the Permanent
Council) headed by the Polish king. Russia never trusted Poniatowski

completely, though, and ambassador Stackelberg supervised his activities closely.

The Russian system in Poland lasted for thirteen years but internal contradictions in Russia's policy eventually brought about its downfall. Panin's rival, Grigorii Potemkin, aimed at redirecting Russian policy toward expansion in the south in alliance with Austria and undermined Panin's plans by supporting elements hostile to the Polish king. Alexander Bezborodko, Catherine II's secretary, supported Potemkin.

An Opposition Party in Poland composed of ministers and rich nobles challenged Stanisław August's dominant position. Secured by a powerful ally in St. Petersburg and occasional gestures from Austria motivated by the desire to win alliance with Russia for a joint policy of Balkan expansion, the Opposition constantly attacked Stanisław August from 1775 to 1788. The Opposition declared in the name of the Sarmatian ideology that the king and the Permanent Council were dangerous to precious Polish liberties and sought to abolish, or at least restrict, their power. Concessions in the form of patronage to prevent the use of the *liberum veto* at the free diets of 1778 and 1780 brought a reduction of Opposition activity for several years, but the confinement of Bishop Soltyk led to a filibuster of the 1782 diet. The Dogrumowa Affairs of 1785 and the stormy 1786 diet were stepping stones to the successful assault on the Permanent Council during the Four Year Diet which began in 1788.

Negative obstructionism characterized the political activities of the republican Opposition coalition. It neither advanced reform programs of its own nor cooperated with the king to pass those measures which would not affect their interests adversely. Since it depended on foreign support, the Opposition was not even a true independence movement, for all its complaints about Russian control. Its leaders understood that Russia dominated Poland and hoped to replace the king as head of the Russian system. In this, they were following the policy of the Czartoryski Party, which contributed the major part of Opposition strength. Hetman Franciszek Branicki went to St. Petersburg twice (with Adam Czartoryski in 1775 and with Igancy Potocki in 1776) to persuade the Russian court to back his party. In 1782, Branicki married Alexandra Engelhardtova in the hope of gaining political concessions. In 1787, members of the Opposition went to Kiev to convince Catherine II to support them. The Opposition also used Austrian support to bolster its attacks on the king. Austria helped it enter the Permanent Council in 1778 and succeeding years and permitted it to paralyze the activities of the diet through filibuster.

The significance of the sterile political wars of 1775-88 can be seen in the dramatic period of the Four Year Diet and the Kościuszko Uprising. The significance lies precisely in that nothing happened at a time when change was of vital importance for national survival. In fact, there was even a slight step backward as the Czartoryski Party, enriched by dynastic alliance with the Potockis and Rzewuskis, became firmly Sarmatian in politics. Historians can see with the advantage of hindsight that the members of the Opposition were far from unified in political orientation. But at that time, family ties seemed far more significant to the individuals involved than did questions of policy. Even the Enlightenment did not create a gulf between the future "true" and "false" patriots. Both adhered to the manners and customs created in France and popularized throughout Europe.

As a result, the progressive alliance which produced the constitution of May 3, 1791 came into existence only in 1790. Had such a reorganization of Polish politics occurred right after the first partition, a comprehensive package of reform legislation might have been written for passage at the first opportunity when Russian control was lifted. Minor reform measures like the king's propositions from the throne and the Zamoyski Law Code might have been passed immediately. Had the alliance between the royal and republican reformers been created in 1788, at the start of the Four Year Diet, there still might have been time to make the necessary changes before the diplomatic situation changed against Poland's interests. In 1790, when Poniatowski and Potocki finally achieved reconciliation, Prussia had lost interest in the alliance with Poland and Russia was on the verge of winning her war against Turkey.

It was too late.

APPENDIX

"Propositions from the Throne" put forward by King Stanislaw August Poniatowski at free diets.

1778: Dyaryusz Seymowy, pp. 33-35

1. Postpone consideration of Zamoyski law code until the next diet.
2. Revise 1776 law on granting credit to landowners in order to prevent excessive borrowing.
3. Regularize the status of estates held in trust for orphans (nobles). Those estates held for more than 50 years will not be questioned.
4. Increase the size of the army.
5. Asks the diet to take over financial responsibility for the Cadet School.
6. Asks thanks and approval for acts of the National Education Commission.
7. Asks approval for king's handling of budget.

1780: Dyaryusz Seymowy, pp. 31-35
1. Requests salaries for deputies to diet.
2. Requests salaries for real estate judges and increase in their numbers.
3. Requests funds for establishment of effective penal system.
4. Asks approval of Permanent Council project for regulating foreign military recruitment on Polish soil.
5. Asks postponement of Zamoyski Code and establishment of a review committee consisting of three senators, the marshal of the diet, and three deputies from the lower house.
6. Asks diet to appropriate new sums for the army; notes king's own contributions.
7. Requests establishment of tobacco monopoly for two years only in order to raise government revenue.
8. Requests annual sum for prospecting for salt.
9. Requests continuation of personnel of National Education Commission at expiry of term.

1782: Dyaryusz Seymowy, pp. 38-41
1. Requests ratification of border demarcation treaty with Russia.
2. Requests support for Jacek Jezierski's discovery of salt springs. No new appropriations necessary.
3. Asks Treasury Commission to take over management of mint from king.
4. Requests more funds for army.
5. Requests increase in number of senators.
6. Asks approval of Permanent Council-prepared bill proposing to use the army to execute court decrees.
7. Requests salaries for deputies to provincial judicial tribunals and funds for city guards and prisons.
8. Asks naturalization with recognition of nobility for several foriegn nobles.

1784: Dyaryusz Seymowy, pp. 40-43

1. Requests approval for commissions which the 1782 diet had not handled.

2. Asks ratification of agreement with Russia concerning use of the port of Riga.

3. Asks ratification of tariff agreement with Russia.

4. Requests higher salary for Marshals of judicial tribunals and some salary for deputies at tribunals, prison guards, and funds for prisons and archives.

5. Requests passage of bill allowing the army to execute court decrees.

6. Requests diet to find new ways to recruit for Polish army and to increase invalids's pensions.

7. Requests citizenship and nobilitation for Princes de Anhalt and de Nassau.

8. Asks diet to find quick way to handle complaints for foreign governments concerning treatment of their citizens in Poland.

9. Requests an increase of number of senators from the Grand Duchy of Lithuania.

1786: AGAD AKP 378, pp. 270-73

1. Requests ratification of agreement with Austria concerning funds from Galician estates of the Diocese of Kraków.

2. Requests ratification of border deliniatation in Silesia with Prussia and requests that losses of certain nobles be made up by the diet.

3. Requests slight revaluation of Polish currency to bring it into line with changes in other European currencies.

4. Requests passage of Permanent Council bill on recruitment.

5. Requests establishment of grain storehouses for use in case of crop shortages.

6. Requests the Crown Provinces to imitate a Lithuanian law permitting the purchase of land by non-noble foreigners.

7. Requests funds for dredging two rivers and building a canal.

8. Requests increased salary for marshal of judicial tribunals and investigation of ways to reduce deputies's expenses.

9. Asks that funds be appropriated for municipal guards so that army troops may be used for their proper duties.

10. Asks investigation of establishing some kind of national bank for granting credit.

NOTES

NOTES TO CHAPTER 1

(1) Jan Stanisław Bystrón, *Dzieje obyczajów w dawnej Polsce* (Warsaw 1960), II, 281.

(2) Stanisław Konarski, *Pisma Wybrane* (Warsaw 1955), I, 228.

(3) Hubert Vautrin in Wacław Zawadzki (ed.), *Polska Stanisławowska w oczach cudzoziemców* (Wrocław 1963), I, 797-99.

(4) Zawadzki, *Polska Stanislawowska*, I, 482, 493-4.

(5) Marian Henryk Serejski (ed.), *Historycy o historii* (Warsaw 1963), I, 36.

(6) Ludwik Bernacki, *Teatr, dramat i muzyka za Stanisława Augusta* (Lwów 1925), I, 36.

(7) Julian Ursyn Niemcewicz, *Pamiętnik czasów moich* (Warsaw 1957), I, 57.

(8) Feliks Oraczewski quoting Montesquieu in Stanisław Tync, *Komisja Edukacji Narodowej. Wybór źródeł* (Wrocław 1954), p. 19.

(9) Quoted in Jean Fabre, *Stanisław-Auguste Poniatowski et l'Europe des lumières* (Paris 1952), p. 256.

(10) Louis-Philippe Ségur, *Mémoires ou souvenirs et anecdotes* (Paris 1844), I, 431.

(11) Jan Kott (ed.). *Poezja polskiego Oświecenia. Antologia* (Warsaw 1956), p. 386.

(12) Stanisław August Poniatowski, *Mémoires du roi Stanislas-Auguste Poniatowski* (Petrograd 1924), II, 278. (Hereafter SAP)

(13) Segur, II, 111-12.

(14) SAP, II, 299.

NOTES TO CHAPTER 2

(1) Stackelberg to Izabella z Czartoryskich Lubomirska, 18 August (1775?), WAPKr APD 151, XXVIII, 1 80; *Sbornik imperatorskogo ruskogo istoricheskogo obshchestva*, CXVIII, 498-500 (hereafter cited as Sirio); S.M. Solovev, *Istoria Rossii s drevneishikh vremen* (Moscow 1960), XV, 170; Konopczyński, *Geneza*, annex 9, p. 385; Herbert H. Kaplan, *The First Partition of Poland* (New York 1962), pp. 183-89.

(2) Konopczyński, *Geneza*, pp. 1-9, 196.

(3) SAP, II, 16-18; J.D. Ochocki, *Pamiętnik angedotyczny z czasów Stanisława Augusta* (Poznań 1867), pp. 84-91; Kazimierz Morawski, ''Prokonsulat Stackelberga'', *Biblioteka Warszawska* LXXXI:2 (1911), 561-2.

(4) 12 April, 25 July, and 7 August 1774, "Entretiens du roi avec le comte de Stackelberg", PAN 1649 (hereafter cited as "Entretiens"); SAP, II, 237; Emanuel Rostworowski, *Ostatni Król Rzeczypospolitej* (Warsaw, 1963), pp. 79-81.

(5) VL, VIII, 23, 33-4, 45.

(6) J. Matuszewski, "Sprzedawalność urzedów w Polsce szlacheckiej", *Czasopismo Prawno-historyczne* XVI:2 (1964), 167.

(7) Tadeusz Manteuffel and others, *Historia Polski* (Warsaw 1958), II, 84; Aleksander Gieysztor and others, *History of Poland* (Warsaw 1968), p. 332.

(8) Helena Waniczkówna, "Adam Czartoryski", *PSB*, IV, 250; Kaplan, p. 28.

(9) Ernst Herrmann, *Geschichte des Russischen Staates* (Gotha 1860), V, 112-4; Rostworowski, *Ostatni*, p. 90.

(10) Konopczyński, *Geneza, pp. 399-402; and Kazimierz Maryan Morawski, "'Dwie rozmowy Stanisława Augusta z Ksawerym Branickim"*, *Rocznik Towarzystwa historycko-literackiego w Paryżu 1868* (Paris 1869), pp. 136-37.

(11) Frederick to Solms, 7 June 1775, *Politische Correspondenz Friedrichs des Grossen*, XXXVII 23, 994 64 (hereafter cited as PC).

(12) Jakubowski to Vergennes, 14 October 1775, AMAE P309; Gunning to Suffolk, 12 23 October 1775, PROSP 91 99; SAP, II, 282-83; Morawski, "Dwie rozmowy", pp. 138-40; Solovev, XV, 184.

(13) Bonneau to Vergennes, 30 September and 7 October 1775, AMAE P309; Gérault to Vergennes, 7 October 1775, AMAE P309; Morawski, "Dwie rozmowy", p. 140.

(14) Gérault to Vergennes, 7 October, 4 November and 25 November, 1775, AMAE P309; Bonneau to Vergennes, 18 October and 25 November, 1775, AMAE P309; Gunning to Suffolk, 12 23 October 1775, PROSP 91 99; "Entretiens", 23 April 1775, "Opis Stanu Rzeczypospolitey Polskiey od Ustawy Rady Nieustajacey w Roku 1775 aż do zaczęcia się Seymu Ordynaryinego w Roku 1776", WAPkr APD D. 236, p. 17 (hereafter cited as "Opis stanu"); Kalinka, *Sejm*, I, 176; and *Korzon*, I, 351.

(15) 12 November 1775, AGAD APP 90; and "Opis stanu", p. 10.

(16) "Opis stanu", p. 8; *HPIP*, II, 544.

(17) This is the origin of the name of one of modern Warsaw's major streets, *Aleje Jerozolimskie* — Jerusalem Boulevard.

(18) "Opis stanu", pp. 15-16; Warszawa Ekonomiczna (AGAD) 542; 22 June 1775 to 30 July 1776; Tymoteusz Lipinski, "Wiadomość o Nowej Jerozolimie" *Biblioteka Warszawska* 1845: 4 pp. 403-07.

(19) "Opis stanu", p. 10, 19; Kalinka, *Sejm*, I, 186-87; Herrmann, V, 106-07.

(20) Gérault to Vergennes, 16 December 1776, AMAE P309; Entretiens", 17, 20, and 30 December 1776); Hermann, V, 106-07.

(21) "Entretiens", 17 and 30 December 1775 and 10 January 1776; Herrmann, V, 123.

(22) Stanisław August to Stackelberg, 6 February 1776, "Changemens survenues dans les affaires du Roi de Pologne depuis l'année 1768", AGAD ZP 172 454.

(23) Deboli to Stanisław August, 30 January 1776, AGAD AKP 70; Kalinka, *Sejm*, I, 174-75.

(24) "Pamiętnik bytnośći w Petersburgu J.W. Branickiego Hetmana W. Kor. y Potockiego Pisarza W. WXL". AGAD APP 313 XII, p. 44 hereafter cited as "Pamiętnik".

(25) "Reflexye, czyli Instrukcye komuś (podobno Marszałkowi Potockiemu) do Petersburga wysłanemu od Partyi Patriotyczney, AGAD APP 313 IX, pp. 24-31; "Punkta do Traktowania w Petersburgu 1776", AGAD APP 313 XII, pp. 50-51.

(26) Quoted in Morawski, *Ignacy Potocki*, p. 45; Stackelberg to Stanisław August, 2 February 1776, AGAD ZP 172; "Pamiętnik", p. 45; Gunning to Suffolk, 8/19 March 1776, PROSP 91 99.

(27) SAP, I, 268.

(28) Deboli to Stanisław August, 8 March 1776, AGAD AKP 70; and "Pamiętnik", p. 47.

(29) "Entretiens", 19 March 1776.

(30) Deboli to Stanisław August, 8 March 1776, AGAD AKP 70.

(31) Bonneau to Vergennes, 13 April 1776, AMAE P309, (copies in AGAD APP 90 237 ff; and AMAE P309 68ff); Morawski, *Ignacy Potocki, p. 46.*

(32) "Entretiens", 23 April 1776; Herrmann, V, 473-74.

(33) 23 February 1776, AGAD APP 90 239.

(34) Lubomirski to Stanisław August, 25 August 1776, AGAD APP 90/250.

(35) Rzewuski to Stanisław August, 28 March, 1776, AGAD APP 90/286; Solovev, XV, 187.

(36) Branicki to Stanisław August, undated, AGAD APP 90/258-59.

(37) 14 and 20 April 1776; Stanisław Poniatowski, "Mémoires du Prince Stanisław Poniatowski", *Revue d'histoire diplomatique*, IX (1895), 491.

(38) "Entretiens", 23 April 1776; Herrmann, V, 473.

(39) Gérault to Vergennes, 11 May 1776, AMAE P309; Reviczky to Princess Lubomirska, 8 June 1776, AGAD APP 90/343-44; SAP, II, 310; Ludwik Dębicki, *Puławy* (Lwow, 1887), I, 35.

(40) Frederick to Benoît, 21 April 1776, PC XXXVIII 24, 674 39.

(41) "Opis stanu", p. 31; "Declaration", 26 July 1776, AMAE P309, SIRIO CXLV, 85, 145.

(42) Bonneau to Vergennes, 28 April 1776, AMAE P309; and Herrmann, V, 118-19.

(43) "List J.W. Xawerego Branickiego Hetmana Wielkiego Koronnego przed Seymikami 13 Junii 1776"; "List Stanisława Lubomirskiego Marszalka Wielkiego Koronnego na seymiki przedseymowe poselskie pisany R. 1776"; "List Wacława Rzewuskiego Woiewody Krakowskiego do Prześwietnych woiewództwu, Ziem, i Powiatów na Seymiki Przedseymowe Poselskiego pisany 1776 r."; "List Seweryna Rzewuskiego Hetmana Polnego Koronnego na seymiki przedseymowe", AGAD APP 90 323-33; and "Opis Stanu", p. 47.

(44) Gérault to Vergennes, 29 July 1776, AMAE P309; Herrmann, V, 120-21.

(45) Solovev, XV, 189-90.

(46) "Relacya seymiku poselskiego Powiatu Słonimskiego 1776 r.", AGAD APP 90, p. 429; "Dyaryusz seymiku wileńskiego", AGAD APP 90, p. 425.

(47) "Opis stanu", pp. 33-35; Herrmann, V, 120.

(48) "Excerpta z Instrukcyi danych Posłom na Seym Ordynaryiny 1776", AGAD ZP 129 26ff, especially Kraków and Sandomierz; and Adolf Pawiński (ed.), *Dzieje ziemi kujawskiej oraz akta historyczne* (Warsaw 1888), V, 291. The Republic continued to use titles from regions which had been partially lost in the seventeenth century: Kiev, Smolensk, Witebsk, Minsk, for example; see Korzon, IV, 38-39.

(49) "Entretiens", 27 July; and 1 August 1776; Stanisław August to Tyzenhauz, 29 July 1776, AGAD APP 310.

(50) Branicki to S. Rzewuski, 19 August 1776, WAPCr AP II 2 5; SAP, II, 324; and *Reprezentacya Ministrów Narodowych Królowi J.K. Mci. Dnia 22 Sierpnia przed Seymem podana,* AGAD APP 90 431-32; Signatories: Branicki, Ogiński, and S. Rzewuski (hetmen); Borch and Chreptowicz (vice-chancellors); Kossowski (treasurer); favorable; Lubomirski (marshall) and Sosnowski (hetman) — the latter is listed inaccurately as a signatory in Jakubowski to Vergennes, 30 August 1776, AMAE P309.

(51) Anonymous, *List szambelana J.K. Mci. o Warszawie przed Seymem,* AGAD APP 313 IX 126-27; Anonymous, *List pewnego Senatora do Obywatela pisany 1776,* AGAD APP 90 27-90; Anonymous, untitled AC 807 379-80.

(52) *DYARYUSZ Seymu Ordinaryinego pod związkiem Konfederacyi generalney Oboyga Narodów agitujacego sie* (Warsaw 1776), p. 2-11 (hereafter cited as *Dyaryusz* (1776); "Opis stanu", p. 46; Solovev, XV, 192; and Niemcewicz, I, 79.

(53) 25 August 1776, AGAD APP 313 IX 79-80; SAP, II, 336; "Opis stanu", p. 51-52; and *Dyaryusz* (1776), p. 29; 51.

(54) *Dyaryusz* (1776), pp. 17-18.

(55) *Dyaryusz* (1776), p. 58.

(56) *Dyaryusz* (1776), p. 70.

(57) *Dyaryusz* (1776), p. 73.

(58) *Dyarusz* (1776), pp. 84-85, 164-68 and 295; VL, VII, 601.

(59) *Obidśnienie Ustanowienia Rady Nieustaacey Przy Boku Waszym,* VL, VIII, 849-50.

(60) *Dyaryusz* (1776), pp, 307-14; *Dyaryusz* (1778), pp. 79-89; *Dyaryusz* (1780), pp. 58-66; *Dyaryusz* (1782), pp. 134-47, *Dyaryusz* (1784), pp. 86-126; VL, VIII, 949-50, 969, and IX, 10-11, 33-34.

(61) *Powinnosci i władza Departamentow w Radzie przy boku naszym Nieustaiacym, oraz tłumaczenie oboiętnosci prawa 1775 ustawy teyże Rady,* VL, VIII, 850-55.

(62) VL, VIII, 859-65, 890-91; Ambroise Jobert, *La Commission d'Education nationale en Pologne* (Paris 1941) pp. 215-16; Korzon, IV, 59.

(63) *Dyaryusz* (1776), p. 109; Kaplan, p. 88.

(64) VL, VIII, 875-76.

(65) VL, VIII, 881-93; Korzon, IV, 19.

(66) VL, VIII, 843; *Dyaryusz* (1776), p. 471.

NOTES TO CHAPTER 3

(1) Stanisław August to Grimm, 10 February 1777, AGAD ZP 221.

(2) SAP, II, 460-62.

(3) Jerzy Michalski, "Dwie misje księcia Stanisława", *Ksiega pamiątkowa 50-lecia Archiwum Glownego Akt Dawnych w Warszawie,* (Warsaw 1958), p. 405.

(4) Husarzewski to Ogrodzki, 21 January 1777 and 8 April 1777, AC 705; Gerault to Vergennes, 7 June 1777, AMAE P309; II, 476-77; Stanisław August to Stanisław Poniatowski, 2 March 1777, AGAD AKP 707; SIRIO CXLV, 377-78; SAP, II, 476-77.

(5) "Entretiens", 10 Feburary and 30 September 1778.

(6) Bonneau to Vergennes, 8 March and 1 August 1777, AMAE P310.

(7) SAP, II, 502.

(8) Wroughton to Suffolk, 8 March 1777, PROSP 88 114; Zofia Libiszowska, *Misja Polska w Londynie* 1769-1795 (Lodz 1966) p. 46; Kaplan, p. 157.

(9) Władysław Konopczynski, *Polska a Turcja* (Warsaw 1935), pp. 258-59; Sirio, CXXXV, 94; Wroughton to Suffolk, March 1777, PROSP 88/114; Gérault to Vergennes, 19 April 1777, AMAE P310; Jakubowski to Vergennes, 23 May 1777, AMAE P310;

(10) Alan W. Fisher, *The Russian Annexation of the Crimea 1772-1783* (Cambridge, England 1970), pp. 74-93ff.; and M.S. Anderson, *The Eastern Question,* 1774-1924 (New York 1966), p. 6; Michalski, "Dwie misje", p. 403.

(11) 21 February 1777, Stanisław August to Boscamp, AGAD 2P 235.

(12) Jan Reychman , *Orient w Kulturze Polskiego Oświecenia* (Wrocław 1969); Gérault to Vergennes, 30 August 1777; AMAE P310; and Bonneau to Vergennes, 13 September 1777, AMAE P310; Wroughton to Suffolk, 10 September 1777, PROSP 88/114; Sirio, CXLV, 455-56.

(13) Anonymous, 5 June 1777, WAPCr AP I 1/118; Reychman, p. 33; Konopczyński, *Polska a Turcja,* pp. 266-67.

(14) Le Bas to Gérard, 17 October 1777, AMAE T163.

(15) Gérault to Vergennes, 19 January 1776, AMAE P309.

(16) Gérault to Vergennes, 19 July 1776, AMAE P309; Bruckner, II, 500; Soloviev, XV, 188; Sirio, XCLV, 470.

(17) Wroughton to Suffolk, 31 August 1776, PROSP 88 114; Leon Rzewuski (ed.), *Kronika Podhorecka* (Kraków 1860), pp. 123-23; SAP, II, 515; Kazimierz Maryan Morawski, "Prokonsulat Stackelberga", *Biblioteka Warszawska,* LXXI:2 (1911), 564.

(18) Vergennes to Gérault, 21 June 1777, AMAE P310.

(19) Eugeniusz Mottaż, (ed.), *Stanisław Poniatowski i Maurycy Glayre, korespondencya dotyczaca rozbiorów Polski,* translated by Jadwiga Baranowski (Warsaw 1901), II, 21-22.

(20) Monet to Vergennes, 2 November 1777, AMAE P310.

(21) 'Entretiens", 3 November 1777; Sirio, CXLV, 504, 513.

(22) Le Bas to Gérard, 17 December 1777, AMAE 163.

(23) Monet to Vergennes, 2 November 1777, AMAE P309; Mottaż, II, 24-26.

(24) "Coup d'oeil sur la Pologne relativement à la France", AMAE P310 216-21.

(25) *Zbiór praw,* p. x; Wybicki, *Życie,* pp. 128, 142-44.

(26). *Zbiór Praw Sądowych na mocy konstytucy; roku 1776 prez JW Andreya Zamoyskiago ex-Kanclerza; Kawalera orla bialego ulozony na seym roku 1778 podany* (Warsaw 1780, part I article XXXI.

(27) *Zbiór praw,* Part I, articles *XXIII-XXV*

(28) *Zbiór praw,* Part I article IV and part III, articles IV and V.

(29) *Zbiór praw,* Part I, article XVI

(30) Mieczysław X. Tarnawski, *Kodeks Zamoyskiego na tle stosunków kościelno-państwowych za czasów Stanisława Augusta* (Lwów 1916), pp. 137-40, 163-64.

(31) AC 721 501, Sandomierz instructions. See also Poznań, Kraków, Lublin, Wilno, Grodno, Smoleńsk, Minsk, Wołyń, and Podole.

(32) "Punkta do Instrukcyi od Obywatelów Poslom na Seym ordynaryiny 1778 podane", AC 721 573-75.

(33) Wybicki, *Życie,* p. 206; Krystyna Adolphowa, "Sprawa Kodeksu Zamoyskiego na seymikach litewskich", *Ksiega pamiątkowa kola historyków słuchaczy Uniwersytetu Stefana Batorege w Wilnie 1923-1933* (Wilno 1933),p. 120; Tarnawski, pp. 157-58.

(34) Mottaż, II, 35; *Dyaryusz* (1778), p. 33.

(35) Wybicki, *Życie,* pp. xi-xii, 155.

(36) Tarnawski, p. 229.

(37) VL, VII, 979.

(38) *Dyaryusz* (1780), pp. 338, 356.

(39) Michał Zaleski, *Pamiętniki Michała Zaleskiego* (Poznań 1879), p. 60; Witold Kula, *Szkice o manufakturach* (Warsaw 1956) I, 427-38; Stanisław Kutrzeba, *Historia Ustroju Polski w Zarysie* (Lwow 1912), I, 235.

(40) M. Zaleski, pp. 88, 98.

(41) "Entretiens", 15 May, 7 November, and 30 November, 1777; SAP, II, 195-96; Sirio CXLV, 392; Adam Naruszewicz, *Korespondencja Adama Naruszewicza 1969-1972* (Warsaw 1959), pp. pp 83-83.

(42) Stanisław August to Benedykt Morykoni, 13 October 1777, AC 721.

(43) SAP, II, 501; Kościalkowski, *Studia,* p. 54.

(44) M. Zaleski, p. 90; Kossakowski, pp. 91-93; Kula, I, 432-33.

(45 SAP, II, 553.

(46) "Entretiens",14 December 1778; Stanisław August to Tyzenhauz, 30 December 1778, 21 January and 23 January 1779 AC 718.

(47) Stanislaw August to Tyszkiewicz, 26 April 1779, AC 702; Jakubowski to Vergennes, 6 March 1779, AMAE P311; M. Zaleski, pp. 119-21.

(48) AC 717, pp. 47-49, 213-20.

(49) Stanisław August to Tyzenhauz, 31 January 1780, AC 718.

(50) Tyzenhauz to Stanisław August, 12 February 1780; Stanisław August to Tyzenhauz, 14 February 1780, AC 718.

(51) Stanisław August to Tyzenhauz, 17 March 1780, AC 718; "Do rozmowy z Jpanem Podskarbim Tyzenhauzem", 21 April 1780 AC 718, "Minut", 27 April 1780, AC 718.

(52) Stanisław August to Tyzenhauz, 26 June 1780, AC 718; Kościałkowski, *Studia,* pp. 58-59.

(53) Stanisław August to Tyzenhauz, 29 June 1780, AC 718; Herrmann, V, 496.

(54) J.I. Kraszewski, *Polska w czasie trzech rozbiorów* (Warsaw 1902), I, 249.

(55) Bonneau to Vergennes, 18 July 1780, AMAE P311; Kula, I, 434.

(56) Stanisław Lubomirski to Ignacy Potocki, 23 August 1780, AGAD APP 279a/211; Kossakowski, pp. 111-12.

(57) Kossakowski, pp. 113-15; M. Zaleski, p. 131.

(58) Kossakowski, p. 116; Anna Kalinkiewiczowna, "Rozkład partii Tyzenhauza na tle sejmików litewskich", *Księga pamiątkowa koła historyków; — słuchaczy Uniwcrsytetu Stefana Batorgo w Wilnie 1923-1933*(Wilno 1933), p. 143.

(59) *DYARYUSZ Seymu wolnego ordynaryinego warszawskiego sześcioniedzielnego R.P. 1780 dnia 2 miesiąca października odprawuiącego się* (Warsaw 1780), p. 168 hereafter cited as *Dyaryusz* (1780), and VL, VIII, pp. 973-74; M. Zaleski, p. 136.

(60) M. Zaleski, pp. 157-58; Stanisław Kościałkowski, "Z literatury polemicznosadowej XVIII wieku", *Ateneum Wileńskie*, V:15 (1928), pp. 8-22.

(61) VL, IX, pp. 12-13; Kościałkowski, *Studia*, p. 61.

(62) Paul B. Bernard, *Joseph II and Bavaria*, (Hague 1965), pp. 48-49, 111.

(63) Husarzewski to Ogrodzki, 20 January 1778, AC 705; Solovev, XV, 239.

(64) Solovev, XV, 239.

(65) Deboli to Stanisław August, 30 December 1777, AGAD AKP 70; Stanisław August to Zablocki, 13 May 1778, PAN 1656.

(66) Cetner to J. Mniszech, 22 April 1778, AC 3873.

(67) Most recently in May 1777: Frederick to Solms, 31 May 1777, PC XXXIX 25, 501 209; Solms to Frederick, 16 May 1777, PC XXXIX 25, 501 209.

(68) Celner to J. Mniszech, 25 April 1778, AC 3873; Abbé de Lisle to J. Mniszech, 13 May 1778, AC 3873.

(69) Blanchot to Frederick, 11 April 1778, PC XL 26, 264 405; Solms to Frederick, 14 April 1778, PC XL 26, 310 458; Blanchot to Frederick, 8 August 1778, PC XLI 26, 626 369; Frederick to Blanchot, 17 August 1778, PC XLI 26 626 369-70.

(70) Frederick to Blanchot, 16 October 1778, PC XLI 26, 761 544-45.

(71) SAP, II, 551-52; and Ogrodzki to Deboli, 19 October 1778, AGAD AKP 70.

(72) Ogrodzki to Deboli, 16 November 1778, AGAD AKP 70; Morawski, "Dwie rozmowy", pp. 54-60 gives the text of this incident, originally from AC 799.

(73) Ogrodzki to Deboli, 19 Oceober 1778, AGAD AKP 70.

(74) Bonneau to Vergennes, 7 April 1779, AMAE P311.

(75) SAP, II, 656; "Korespondencja Zabłockiego", 17 September 1779, PAN 1656; and Gérault to Vergennes 18 September 1779, AMAE P311; Jakubowski to Vergennes 27 October 1779 AMAE P311; Jerzy Michalski, *Polska wobec wojny o sukcesję bawarską* (Warsaw 1964), p. 26-27. See also Zbigniew Szczęska. "Sad Sejmowy w okresie Rady nieustajacej, Proces barona Juliusa", *Przeglad Historyczny* LXII (1971); 3,421-36.

(76) Bonneau to Vergennes, 3 January 1780, AMAE P311; Axt to Frederick, 3 January 1780, PC XLIV 27, 765 22; Frederick to Axt, 12

January 1780, PC XLIV 27, 765 22; Frederick to Goertz, 8 January 1780, PC XLIV 27, 760 14; Goertz to Frederick, 4 February 1780, PC XLIV 27, 831 84-85.

(77) Jerzy Michalski, "Do dziejów stronnictwa autriackiego i polskiej polityki po I rozbiorze", *Księga pamiątkowa ku uczczeniu sicdemdziesiatej rocznicy urodzin prof. dra Janusza Wolińskiego* (Warsaw 1954), p. 142.

(78) Bonneau to Vergennes, 6 May 1780, AMAE P311; Cieciszowski to Deboli, 8 May 1780, AGAD AKP 263; Stanisław August to Deboli, 9 July 1780, AGAD AKP 263.

(79) AGAD AKP 89.

(80) Stanisław Poniatowski, p. 496.

(81) Michalski, "Dwie misje", pp. 413-14.

(82) Cieciszowski to Deboli, 31 May 1780, AGAD AKP 273; Bonneau to Vergennes, 10 June 1780, AMAE P311.

(83) "Entretiens", 13 November 1776 and 18 February 1778,

(84) "Kopia responsu J.O. Xcia Jmci. Lubomirskiego Marszałka W.K. na list okólny J.K. Mci. danego 22 Aprilis 1778", WAPKr AP I 1 118; "List J.O. Wacława Rzewuskiego Woiewody krakowskiego na seymiki poselskie R.P. 1778", AGAD APP 313 IX 218-19; "Punkta do Instruckyi od Obywatelów Posłom na seym ordynaryiny 1778 podane'5, AC 721 573-75.

(85) Naruszewicz to Stanisław August, 23 August 1778, AC 721; Jakubowski to Vergennes, 26 August 1778, AMAE P311; Wacław Rzewuski to Mlodziejowski, undated, WAPKr AP II 2 95; and *Kronika Podhorecka*, p. 125.

(86) Stępkowski to Stanislaw August, 23 August 1778, AC 710.

(87) AC 721 501, 585.

(88) VL, VII, 599.

(89) *Dyaryusz* (1778), pp. 5-10.

(90) *Dyaryusz* (1778), p. 287.

(91) Stanisław August to Michał Ogiński, 29 December 1778, AC 680.

(92) Stanisław August to Monet, 24 November 1778, AMAE P311; Bonneau to Vergennes, 11 November 1778, AMAE P311.

(92) *Dyaryusz* (1778), p. 283; Władysław Konopczyński, *Liberum Veto* (Cracow 1918), p. 423.

(94) Jakubowski to Vergennes, 30 October 1778, AMAE P311.

(95) *Dyaryusz* (1778), pp. 21, 347.

(96) *Dyaryusz*, pp. 131, 157-58ff.

(97) *Dyaryusz*, pp. 49-55, 183-84.

(98) VL, VIII, 956. Following the Czartoryski reforms of 1764, the Fundamental Laws of 1768 recognized two classes of legislation: "matters of state" to which the unanimity rule applied, and "economic matters" which were decided by majority vote. VL, VIII, 595, 953, 957-58.

(99) Bonneau to Vergennes, 8 December 1778, AMAE P311; "Entretiens", 17 December, 23 December 1778.

(100) Bonneau to Vergennes, 12 February 1780, AMAE P311; Branicki to S. Rzewuski, n.d., WAPkr AP 2/5.

(101) *Archiv der Familie von Stackelberg,* (St. Petersburg 1898), I, 87-88.

(102) "Entretiens", 20 September 1778; Bonneau to Vergennes, 20 September 1778 and 13 October 1778, AMAE P311; Stanisław August to

Lubomirski, 1 January 1780, AGAD APP 84; Bonneau to Vergennes, 13 October 1780, AMAE P311; Chreptowicz to Karol Radziwiłł, 5 September 1780, AGAD Arch Radz V, L:50 2181; Chreptowicz to Deboli, 18 September 1780, AGAD AKP 263.

(103) "Listy króla Stanisława Augusta do Szczęsnego Potockiego z lat 1768-1792", *Rocznik Towarzystwa Historycko-literackiego*, III, 261-62.; VL, VIII, 969-76.

(105) *Dyaryusz*, p. 453.

(106) Mottaż, II, 45-46.

(107) Julian Ursyn Niemcewicz, *Pamiętniki czasów moich* (Warsaw 1957), I, 136.

NOTES TO CHAPTER 4

(1) Stanisław August to Antoni Sulkowski, 6 December 1780, AC 713; Mottaz, II, 46-47.

(2) Harris to Stormont, 25 August 5 September, PROSP 91 100; Cieciszowski to Deboli, 20 September 1780; AKP 263; Goertz to Frederick, 19 September 1780, PC XLV 486.

(3) Jakubowski to Vergennes, 12 December 1780, AMAE P311; Blanchot to Frederick, 23 February 1780, PC XLVI 29, 387 520; J.I. Kraszewski *Polska w czasie trzech rozbiorów* (Warsaw 1902), I, 266; Herrmann, V, 132; David Mark Griffiths, "Russian Court Politics and the Question of an Expansionist Foreign Policy under Catherine II, 1762-1783" (unpublished Ph.D. dissertation, Cornell University, 1967), p. 203.

(4) Joseph to Catherine, 21 May 1781, Arneth (ed.), *Joseph II und Katharina von Russland,* pp. 72-80; Catherine to Joseph, 24 May 1781, pp. 81-90.

(5) Griffiths, pp. 202-03; Isabel de Madariaga, *Britain, Russia, and the Armed Neutrality of 1780* (New Haven 1962), pp. 344-45.

(6) Griffiths, pp. 238-44, 263-64.

(7) James Harris, Earl of Malmesbury, *Diaries and Correspondence of James Harris* (London 1845), I, 382, 390; Griffiths, pp. 154-55, 160ff., 178-81; Madariaga, *Britain,* p. 346.

(8) Catherine to Stackelberg, 25 January 1781, letter No. XV, "Pismo Ekateriny II k grafu Stakelberg, 1773-1795", *Russkaia Starina,* III No. 1 (1871), pp. 322-23.

(9) "Conversations du comte Stackelberg avec le roi", 3, 4, 5, 6 March 1781, AGAD AKP 90 10, pp. 9-10.

(10) Stanisław August to Deboli, 16 April 1781, AGAD AKP 261; Stanisław August to Adam Czartoryski, 3 May 1781, AC 719.

(11) Stanisław August to Cieciszowski, 24 November 1781, AGAD ZP 210; Stanisław August to Deboli, 24 December 1781, AGAD AKP 263; Niemcewicz, I, 144-45.

(12) Korzon, IV, 290. Although Engelhardtova's relationship to Catherine II and Potemkin has not been proved, her marriage was certainly regarded by contemporaries as a significant political act.

(13) Deboli to Stanisław August, 19 January 1781, AGAD AKP 262; "Conversations du comte Stackelberg avec le roi", 11 March 1781, AGAD AKP 90/10, p. 10.

(14) Frederick to Buchholtz, 8 April 1781, PC XLV 28, 671/369.

(15) "Conversations du comte Stackelberg avec le roi", 12 April 1781, AGAD AKP 90/10.

(16) Frederick to Buchholtz, 25 July 1781, PC XLVI 28, 911/66, Griffiths, pp. 197-99.

(17) Gérault to Vergennes, 13 October 1781, AMAE P311; *Joseph II und Ludwig Cobenzl, Ihr Briefwechsel* (Vienna 1901), I, 211.

(18) Cieciszowski to Deboli, 24 September 1781, AGAD AKP 263.

(19) Stanisław August to Cieciszowski, 31 October 1781, AGAD ZP 210; Cieciszowski to Deboli, 12 November 1781, AGAD AKP 263. Frederick to Buchholtz, 18 November 1781 PC XLVI 29, 143 278; Sirio, IX, 90.

(20) Bonneau to Vergennes, 1 February 1782, AMAE P312 and Catherine to Stackelberg, 19 August 1782, letters No. XVIII and XIX, "Pisma Ekateriny II k grafu Stakelbergu", *Russaia Starina*, III:1, 323-24; Gérault to Vergennes, 3 July 1782, AMAE P 312.

(21) Stanisław August to Deboli, 14 January 1782, AGAD AKP 66; Tomasz Ostrowski *Poulne Wieści z Oświeconej Warszawy* (Warsaw 1972), pp. 131, 137.

(22) Gérault to Vergennes, 2 February 1782, AMAE P312; Stanisław Grodzisko, *Obywatelstwo szlacheckiej Rzeczypospolitej* (Cracow 1963), pp. 189-90.

(23)"Rozmowa Stanisława Augusta z Marszałkiem Lubomirskim", 17 February 1782, AGAD ZP 126; Thugut to S. Rzewuski, 10 March 1782, WAPkr AP II/2 131.

(24) Stanisław August to Deboli, 16 April 1781, AGAD AKP 263; Kazimierz Rudnicki, *Biskup Kajetan Sołtyk 1715-1788* (Warsaw 1906) pp. 192-99.

(25) Stanisław August to Deboli, 11 February 1782, AGAD AKP 266; Cieciszowski to Deboli, 10 April 1782, AGAD ZP 126; *Rezolucye Rady względem materyi krakowskiey na sessyach niżey wyrażonych zapadłe, co do słowa wypisane*, 15 February, 26 February and 9 April, 1782, AGAD ZP 120; (hereafter cited as *Rezolucye*), Rudnicki, pp. 201-14; Chamcówna, *Kołłątaj*, pp. 138-44; Schmitt, III, 66-67; Ostrowski, 66-7ff., 97, 114, 118, 251.

(26) *Rezolucye*, 9 April 1782, AGAD ZP 126; Bonneau to Vergennes, 13 April 1782, AMAE P312; Seweryn Rzewuski to Stanisław August, 8 March 1782, AGAD APP 313/XI 180-81; see also AGAD APP 313/XII 147-55; Lubomirski to S. Rzewuski, 14 March 1782, WAPCr II/2 61; and Rudnicki, pp. 218-25.

(27) Stanisław August to Deboli, 4 March 1782, AGAD AKP 266; Frederick to Buchholtz, 13 March 1782, PC XLVI 29, 409/542-43; Rudnicki, p. 226.

(28) Stanisław Potocki to Ignacy Potocki, 21 March 1782, AGAD AKP 279a/329; Stanisław August to Deboli, 4 March 1782, AGAD AKP 266; Gérault to Vergennes, 18 March 1782, AMAE P312; Rudnicki, p. 227.

(29) Deboli to Stanisław August, 22 March, 23 April 1782, 16 August, AGAD APP 265; Gérault to Vergennes, 6 May 1782, AMAE P312.

(30) Deboli to Stanisław August, 16 August and 3 September 1782, AGAD AKP 265; Ostrowski, pp. 153-54.

(31) VL, IX, 1 and 5; Bonneau to Vergennes, 6 July 1782, AMAE P312. Michał Poniatowski, Michał Mniszech, Ludwik Tysziewicz; and Andrzej Mokronowski were related to Stanislaw August — the last three by marriage.

(32) *DYARYUSZ Seymu wolnego ordynaryinego warszawskiego sześcioniedzielnego r.* p. 1782 (Warsaw 1782), pp. 39-41; Cieciszowski to 1782, AGAD AKP 266; Korzon, III, 52.

(33) *Dyaryusz* (1782). 180-230.

(34) *Dyaryusz* (1782), pp. 236-45.

(35) *Dyaryusz*(1782), pp. 329, 343, 364-65, 391, 396.

(36) *Dyaryusz* (1782), pp. 39-41.

(37) *Dyaryusz* (1782), p. 412.

(38) *Dyaryusz* (1782), p. 414.

(39) "Opisanie Seymu", 11 November 1782, AGAD ZP 126; Gérault to Vergennes, 26 October 1782, AMAE P312.

(40) Herrmann, V, 482, Kraszewski, I, 280.

(41) "Opisanie seymu", 11 November 1782, AGAD ZP 126.

(42) "Rozmowa króla z Stanisławem Potockim Podstolim Koronnym 26 September 1782", AGAD ZP 126, 205-06.

(43) "Rozmowa króla z pisarzem Potockim", AGAD ZP 126 207.

(44) Cieciszowski to Deboli, 30 September 1782, AGAD AKP 266; *Dyaryusz* (1782), p. 340; Morawski, *Ignacy Potocki,* p. 122; Waleryan Kalinka, *Ostatnie lata Stanisława Augusta*(Cracow 1891), I, CCLXIV.

(45) Stanisław August to Deboli, 20 October 1782, AGAD AKP 266; VL, IX, 4-5 and *Dyaryusz* (1782), pp. 39-40.

(46) Dalrymple to Gratham, undated (November 1782), PROFO 62/1 43-44.

(47) Deboli to Stanisław August, 12 November, 15 November, and 19 November 1782, AGAD AKP 265.

(48) Bonneau to Vergennes, 1 January 1783, AMAE P312; Kraszewski, I, 273-75.

(49) Niemcewicz, I, 153; Bonneau to Vergennes, 9 May 1783, AMAE P. 312.

(50) Deboli to Stanisław August, 19 November and 20 December 1782, AGAD AKP 265; Stanisław August to Deboli, 24 March, 31 March, and 2 April 1783, AGAD AKP 266.

(51) Stanisław August to Deboli, 16 June 1783, AGAD AKP 266;) Deboli to Stanisław August, 8 July 1783, AGAD AKP 265.

(52) Fisher, pp. 136-37.

(53) Bonneau to Vergennes, 23 May and 26 July 1783, AMAE P312; Stanisław August to Deboli, 28 August and 4 October 1783, AKAE AKP 266.

(54) Stanisław August to Deboli, 7 January 1784, AGAD AKP 266. see also W. Sidorowicz, "Walka o moskiewski aliens", *Polityka Narodów* VIII:3 (1936), 256-82.

(55) Stanisław August to Deboli, 7 January 1783, AGAD AKP 268; Deboli to Stanisław August, 20 January, 30 January, and 6 February 1784, AGAD AKP 267.

(56) Stanisław August to Deboli, 21 April 1783, 25 February, 17 March, 18 May 1784, AGAD AKP 268; Bonneau to Vergennes, 17 March, 1784, AMAE P313; Branicki to S. Rzewuski, 7 June 1784, WAPKr Arch Podh, II 2/5.

(57) Stanisław August to Szczęsny Potocki, 29 July 1784, AC 735; Bronisław Zaleski (ed.), *Korespondencja Krajowa Stanisława Augusta z lat 1784 do 1792* (Poznan 1872), p. 26.

(58) Chreptowicz to Stanisław August, 16 June and 28 June 1784, AC 724; Stanisław August to Szczesny Potocki, 1 July 1784, AC 735.

(59) Stanisław August to Deboli, 21 August 1784, and 9 September 1784, AGAD AKP 268; Aubert to Vergennes, 9 September 1784, AMAE P313; Jakubowski to Vergennes, 21 September 1784, AMAE P313; WAPkr Arch Sang 1035.

(60) Deboli to Stanisław August, 17 August 1784, AGAD AKP 267.

(61) Stanisław August to Deboli, 18 February 1784, AGAD AKP 268.

(62) Adam St. Naruszewicz *Dyaryusz podróży Nayiaśnieyszego Stanisława Augusta Króla Polskiego na Seym Grodzieński zaczqwszy od dnia wyiazdu z Warszawy to iest 26 miesiąca Sierpnia Roku 1784 ał do przybycia do Grodna* (Warsaw 1784), p. i.

(63) B. Zaleski, pp. 32-33; Schmitt, III, 80.

(64) Bonneau to Vergennes, 13 November 1784, AMAE P313; Aubert to Vergennes, 13 November 1784, AMAE, 313.

(65) Bonneau to Vergennes, 13 November 1784, AMAE P313; B. Zaleski, p. 32.

(66) Stanisław August to Deboli, 15 November 1784, AGAD AKP 268; Kazimierz Morawski, *Ignacy Potocki,* pp. 124-25.

(67) Stanisław August to Deboli, 15 November 1784, AGAD AKP 268; Stanisław August to Szczęsny Potocki, 15 January 1785, AC 735; Aubert to Vergennes, 4 November 1784, AMAE P313; B. Zaleski, pp. 34-37.

(68) VL, IX, 12; Bartłomiej Michałowski, "Zapiski Mikhalovskago", *Drevnaia i Novaia Rossaia* XVI, 689.

(69) Bonneau to Vergennes, 20 October 1784, AMAE P313; Aubert to Vergennes, 8 November 1784, AMAE P313.

(70) *DYARYUSZ Seymu wolnego ordynaryinego grodzieńskiego sześcioniedzielnego r. p. 1784 dnia 4 miesiaca pazdziernika odprawuiącego się* (Warsaw 1784). pp. *250ff:* VL, IX, 12-14.

(71) VL, IX, 23-24.

(72) VL, IX, 11-24.

(73) VL, VIII, 945-82 and IX, 1-45; Bonneau to Vergennes, 11 December 1784.

(74) Quoted in Nikolai Ivanovich Kostamarov, *Posliedniie gody Riechipospolitei* (Petersburg 1870), p. 133.

NOTES TO CHAPTER 5

(1) Deboli to Stanisław August, 30 November 1784, AGAD AKP 267.

(2) Bonneau to Vergennes, 11 December 1784, AMAE P313.

(3) Adam Naruszewicz *Sprawa między Xieciem Adamem Czartoryskim Generałem Ziem Podolskich a Janem Komarzewskim Generałem Majorem Przy boku J.K. Mci. i Franciszkiem Ryxem Starostą Piaseczyńskim Kamerdynerem królewskim Oskarżonemi iakoby o zamysł strucia tego xiecia* (Warsaw 1785), pp. 1-72, Stanisław August to Deboli, 19 January and 23 February 1785, AGAD AKP 268.

(4) Dzierzanowski to S. Rzewuski, 21 January 1785, WAPkr AP II 2/28.

(5) Stanisław August to Chreptowicz, 10 July 1784, AC 724; Aubert to Vergennes, 9 October 1784, AMAE P313.

(6) Catherine to Stackelberg, 2 December 1784, XX, Catherine II, ''Pisma Ekateriny II k grafu Stakelbergu'', Ruskaia Starina III (1871), 324-25; Archiv der Familie von Stackelberg, p. 90; Joseph to Cobenzl, Joseph II und Ludwig Cobenzl, Ihr Briefwechsel, II, 27.

(7) Bonneau to Vergennes, 29 January 1785, AMAE P313; Aubert to Vergennes, 14 February 1785, AMAE P313; Stanisław August to Deboli, 9 February and 23 February 1785, AGAD AKP 268.

(8) Deboli to Stanisław August, 1 February 1785, AGAD AKP 267; Aubert to Vergennes, 23 April 1785, AMAE P313; Ségur, Mémoires, I, 437.

(9) Deboli to Stanisław August, 4 March 1785, AGAD AKP 267.

(10) Deboli to Stanisław August, 1 February 1785, and 22 February, AGAD AKP 267; Stanisław August to Deboli, 26 February 1785, AGAD AKP 268; Stackelberg to Aleksandra Engelhardtova Branicka, 20 March 1785, AC 702; Michał Poniatowski to Adam Czartoryski, 26 March 1785, AC 920.

(11) AGAD AKP 95 94-95; Naruszewicz, Sprawa, pp. 69-193.

(12) Stanisław August to Deboli, 16 April 1785, AGAD AKP 268.

(13) Naruszewicz, Sprawa.

(14) Premier éclaircissement réel sur le procès du Prince General de Podolie, AC 901, pp. 638-42.

(15) Anonymous, Observation d'un Polonois impartial sur l'arrêt rendu a Varsovie le 15 Mars 1785(Warsaw 1785), p. 15.

(16) Listy polskie pisane w roku 1785 wydane przez Jana Wit(Warsaw 1785) pp. 371-72. Authorship established by Władysław Semkowicz, Przewodnik po zbiorze rekopisów wilanowskich (Warsaw 1961), p. 187.

(17) Aubert to Vergennes, 9 June 1785, AMAE P314; Libiszowska, p. 72.

(18) Adam Czartoryski to Stanisław August, 22 March 1785, AC 920; Michał Poniatowski to Adam Czartoryski, 26 March 1785, AC 920; Adam Czartoryski to Michał Poniatowski, 26 March 1785, AC 920; Stanisław August to Adam Czartoryski, 26 March 1785, AC 902; Debicki, Puławy, pp. 54-55.

(19) Stanisław August to Deboli, 25 May and 1 June 1785, AGAD AKP 268.

(20) Stanisław August to Deboli, 16 April 1785, AGAD AKP 268; Aubert to Vergennes, 23 April 1785, AMAE P313.

(21) Dzierzanowski to S. Rzewuski, 17 May 1785, WAPCr AP II 2/28; Stanisław August to Deboli, 25 May and 28 May 1785, AGAD AKP 265; Bonneau to Vergennes, 6 June 1785, AMAE P313.

(22) Stanisław August to Deboli, 27 April and 7 May, 1785, AGAD AKP 268.

(23) Catherine to Stackelberg, 25 June 1785, letter XXIV, ''Pisma Ekatoriny II k grafu Stakelbergu'', Russkaia Starina, III, 475; and Archiv der Familie von Stackelberg, I, 91.

(24) Stanisław August to Chreptowicz, 14 September 1785, AC 724; and B. Zaleski, p. 46; Stanisław August to Deboli, 5 September and 14 September 1785, AGAD AKP 268.

(25) Stanisław August to Deboli, 4 March 12 and April 786, AGAD AKP 378; Aubert to Vergennes, 22 March 1786, AMAE P314; Bonneau to Vergennes, 4 April 1786, AMAE P314.

(26) Stanisław August to Deboli, 12 April 1786, AGAD AKP 378.

(27) Stanisław August to Stanisław Poniatowski, 26 April 1786, AC 735.

(28) Ignacy Potocki to Seweryn Rzewuski, 16 June 1786, WAPkr AP II 2/5.

(29) Deboli to Stanisław August, 28 March, 20 June, and 23 June 1786, AGAD AKP 269.

(30) Aubert to Vergennes, 12 September 1786; Stanisław August to Deboli, 13 September 1786, AGAD AKP 378; B. Zaleski, pp. 54-63.

(31) Karol Stanisław Radziwiłł, *Korespondencja Ksiecia Karola Stanisława Radziwiłła wojewody wileńskiego, "panie kochanku" 1744-1790 z archiwum w Werkach,* (Krakow 1898), edited by Czesław Jańkowski, pp. 227-28, 233.

(32) Radziwiłł, p. 227-30; Aubert to Vergennes, 4 October 1785, AMAE 314; Kiciński to Deboli, 14 October 1786, AGAD AKP 378; *Dyaryusz Seymu ordynaryinego warszawsiego Roku 1786 pod laska marszałka Gadomskiego,* AGAD APP 102 (hereafter cited as *Dyaryusz* (1786).

(33) Radziwiłł, p. 232; Cieciszowski to Deboli, 14 October 1786, AGAD AKP 378; Aubert to Vergennes, 21 October 1786, AMAE P314; Stanisław August to Deboli, 1 November 1786, AGAD AKP 378; VL, IX, 30-31.

(34) *Dyaryusz* (1786), 4 November and 6 November 1786.

(36) Speech by Szczęsny Potocki, 24 October 1785 AGAD ZP 105; Stanisław August to Deboli, 1 November 1786, AGAD AKP 378; VL, IX, 34-35; AGAD Ksiegi Kanclerskie 45/46, pp. 45-46. Kobylecki to S. Rzewuski, 18 October 1786, WAPKr AP II 2/41; Rostworowski, *Sprawa,* pp. 154-58, 169, Julian Bartoszewicz, *Znakomici mężowie XVIII wieku* (St. Petersburg 1858), II, 335, 363-64.

(37) Speeches by Suchorzewski, Jabłonowski, and S. Rzewuski, 2 November 1786 and by K.N. Sapieha, 3 November 1786, AGAD AP 105; Bonneau to Vergennes, 4 November 1786, AMAE P314; Stanisław August to Deboli, 11 November 1786, AMAE P314; and VL, IX, 35.

(38) Stanisław August to Deboli, 11 November 1786, AGAD AKP 378.

(39) 3 November and 7 November 1786, AGAD ZP 105; 20 October 1786, AGAD ZP 105.

(40) Stanisław August to Deboli, 1 November and 11 November 1786, AGAD AKP 378.

(41) Stanisław August to Deboli, 11 November 1786, AGAD AKP 378; Niemcewicz, I, 241.

(42) Mottaż, II, 54.

(43) Bonneau to Vergennes, 15 November 1786, AMAE P314.

(44) Ignacy Potocki to S. Rzewuski, 16 November 1786, WAPKr, APII 2/5; Bonneau to Vergennes, 15 November and 20 December 1786, AMAE P314; and Niemcewicz, I, 241.

(45) Deboli to Stanisław August, 4 November 1786, AGAD AKP 269; Kalinka, *Sejm,* I, 66-68; and Łojek, *Misja,* pp. 27-29.

(46) Stanisław August to Deboli, 22 November 1786, AGAD AKP 378; Komarzewski to Stanisław August, 5 December 1786, AGAD AKP 269; Bonneau to Vergennes, 27 January 1787, AMAE P314; AGAD AKP 378, p. 259; Catherine to Stackelberg, 2 December 1786, letter No. XXXI, "Pisma

Ekateriny Vtoroi k grafu Stakelbergu'', *Russkaia Starina* III, 479; Sirio, XXVI, 176.

(47) Catherine to Stackelberg, 2 December 1786, letter No. XXXI ''Pisma Ekateriny Vtoroi k grafu Stakelbergu'', *Russkaia Starina* III, 479; and J.I. Kraszewski (ed.), *Podróż króla Stanisława Augusta do Kaniowa w.r. 1787 podług listów Kazimierza Konstantego Hrabiego de Brol Platera* (Wilno 1860), p. 9 (hereafter cited as Podłoż).

(48) Kraszewski, *Podróż*, p. 187.

(49) Stanisław August to Deboli, 3 January 1787, AGAD AKP 378; Bonneau to Vergennes, 31 March 1787, AMAE P314; Marquis d'Aragon, *Un Paladin au XVIII siècle* (Paris 1893), p. 136; Alexander Visilevich Khrapovickii, *Dnevnik A.V. Khrapovickogo* (Petersburg 1874), p. 28, Niemcewicz, I, 251 speculated that Potemkin might set up an independent kingdom joining his Polish and Russian estates or seek Polish office. See Robert H. Lord, *The Second Partition of Poland* (Cambridge, Mass., 1915), pp. 312-16.

(50) Cérenville, *Memoirs of Prince Potemkin* (London 1813), p. 12.

(51) AGAD AKP 378, p. 244; Sirio, XXVI, 180; Niemcewicz, I, 251; Kalinka, *Ostatnie*, II, 18.

(52) Kalinka, *Ostatnie*, I, CCCIX.

(53) Kalinka, *Ostatnie*, I, CCCVIII.

(54) Bonneau to Vergennes, 21 March and 9 May 1786, AMAE P314; Piattoli to S. Rzewuski, 17 April 1786, WAPKr AP II 2/5; Mottaż, II, 36-37.

(55) Ségur, II, 180.

(56) Mottaż, II, 59.

(57) Radziwiłł, pp. 246-47.

(58) Kalinka, *Ostatnie*, II, 27. This volume contains letters between Pius Kicinski, head of the King's cabinet, and Stanisław August.

(59) Kalinka, *Ostatnie*, II, 23, 25.

(60) Whitworth to Carmarthen, 29 April 1787, PROFO 62/2.

(61) Jan Komarzewski, *Coup d'oeil rapide sur les causes réelles de la décadence de la Pologne* (Paris 1807), p. 194; and Kalinka, *Ostatnie*, II, 33-35.

(62) Ségur, II, 178.

(63) Ségur, II, 178; Jean Henri Castéra, *Vie de Catherine II* (Paris 1797), II, 324-26; Sirio, XXVI, 180.

(64) Stanisław August Poniatowski, *Pamiętniki Stanisława Augusta Poniatowskiego i jego korespondencja z cesarzowa Katarzyną II* (Poznan 1862), II, 97-99.

(65) Kalinka, *Ostatnie*, II, 36.

(66) Sirio, XXVI, 180-82.

(67) Niemcewicz, I, 251; and Kalinka, *Ostatnie*, II, 37-38.

(68) Sirio, XXVI, 182; and Kalinka, *Ostatnie*, II, 39.

(69) Charles, Prince de Ligne, *Mèmories et mélanges historiques* (Paris 1827), I, 53.

(70) Mottaż, II, 58-59.

(71) Radwiwiłł, p. 265.

(72) Charles, Prince de Ligne, *Mèmoires et mélanges historiques* (Paris 1827), I, 53.

(73) Łojek, *Misja*, pp. 29-30; Kalinka, *Sejm*, I, 68-70; and Rostworowski, *Ostatni*, 130-31.

(74) Łojek, *Misja*, p. 35; Kalinka, *Sejm*, p. 69; and Jerzy Michalski, ''Sejmiki poselskie 1788 roku; *Kwartalnik Historyczny*, LI (1960), p. 68 (hereafter cited as Michalski, ''Sejmiki'').

(75) Łojek, *Misja*, pp. 35-36; Kalinka, *Sejm*, pp. 72-75; and Michalski, ''Sejmiki'', pp. 59-60.

(76) Kalinka, *Sejm*, pp. 75-78; Rostworowski, *Ostatni*, 133-36; and Lord, pp. 315-16.

(77) Kalinka, *Sejm*, pp. 100-07; Lord, 88; and Rosworowski, *Ostatni*, pp. 138-41.

(78) Michalski, ''Sejmiki'', pp. 331-64, 465-66; B. Zaleski, pp. 83-105; Kalinka, *Sejm*, I, 148-53; and Rosworowoski, *Ostatni*, pp. 144-47.

(79) Kalinka, *Sejm*, I, 169-70.

(80) Kalinka, *Sejm*, I, 51-65, 114-15; and Lord, pp. 75-78, 89-90.

(81) Kalinka, *Sejm*, I, 193-205ff; Lord, 90-102; Rostworoski, *Ostatni*, 148-50; and Szymon Askenazy, *Przymierze Polsko-pruskie* (Warsaw 1918), pp. 52-58.

(82) Rostworowski, *Sprawa*, pp. 210, 224-27ff; Rostworowski, *Ostatni*, pp. 144-50.

(83) Rostworowski, *Ostatni*, 144-54.

NOTES TO CHAPTER 6

(1) ''Póki Polacy sukni swej się nie wstydzili/Był kraj cały. Polacy dobrze się też mieli/Długi kontusz i długie miał w kraju granice./Dziś Polak w krótkim fraczku krótkie ma ziemie.'' Juliusz Nowak, *Satyra Polityczna Sejmu Czteroletniego* (Cracow 1933), p. 103.

(2) Waleryan Kalinka, *Sejm Czteroletni* (Cracow 1895), I, 606, 640.

(3) Kalinka, *Sejm Czteroletni* I, 629.

(4) Emanuel Rostworowski, *Legendy i Fakty XVIII Wieku* (Warsaw, 1963), pp. 316-18.

(5) Czesław Nanke, *Szlachta wołyńska wobecz Konstytucji trzeciego maja* (Lwów 1907), p. 21; and Kalinka, *Sejm Czteroletni* II, 637.

(6) Władysław Smoleński, *Ostatni Rok Sejmu Wielkiego* (Cracow 1897), p. 420.

(7) Smolenski, *Ostatni Rok*, pp. 5-49.

(8) Smolenski, *Ostatni Rok*, pp. 49-79.

NOTES TO CHAPTER VII

(1) Robert Howard Lord, *The Second Partition of Poland* (Cambridge, Mass, 1915), p. 491.

BIBLIOGRAPHY

ARCHIVAL SOURCES
Kraków, Poland

Archiwum Czartoryskich   Czartoryski Archive

catalogue number   *title*
659   Korespondencja króla
680   Korespondencja Króla
708   Korespondencja króla z Xiężną Sapieżyną
709   Korespondencja króla ze Stępkowskim
710   Korespondencja króla ze Stępkowskim
712   Korespondencja króla z Xciem Augustem i Franciszkiem
         Sułkowskimi 1755-1780
713   Korespondencja króla z Xciem Augustem i Frenciszkiem
         Sułkowskimi 1780-1784
716   Korespondencja króla z Tyzenhauzem
717   Korespondencja króla z Tyzenhauzem
718   Korespondencja króla z Tyzenhauzem
719   Korespondencja króla z Tyzenhauzem
720   Korespondencja króla z Tyzenhauzem
721   Korespondencja króla z Tyzenhauzem
724   Korespondencja Polska
735   Korespondencja Polska
849   Listy króla do Bukatego posła w Anglii 1781-1793
850   Tyzenhauza proces i pisma różne a krolem
920   Korespondencja Polska
959   Podróż kroła z Warszaway na Sejm Grodzieński 1784
961   Rozmowy z posłem rossyjskim (1771) i z nuncjuszami 1772-1778
1984   Odpisy z Public Record Office 1764-1799
1997   Odpisy z Archives des affaires etrangeres
1998   Odpisy z Archives des affaires etrangeres
2258   Listy 1763-1798 dotyczace stosunki polsko-rossyjskie
3172   Szczesny Potocki. Bruliony korespondencji
3872   Korespondencja J. Mniszka z Celnerem
         Polska Akademia Nauk Polish Academy of Sciences
1133   Papiery Sołtyków z lat 1760-1813
1656   Korespondencja Bernarda Zablockiego z gabinetem Króla z lat 1772-
         1779
1649   Entretiens du roi avec le comte de Stackelberg
Województwie Archiwum Państowowe   Provincial State Archives
Archiwum Podhoreckie Podhorec Archive
I 1/118   Materiały o charakterze publicznym 1773-1779

II 2/5 Materialy
Archiwum Potockich (Domowe) Potocki Archives (Home)
151/11 List od Stackelberga do Isabelli Lubomirskiej
D. 236 Opis Stanu Rzeczypospolitey Polskiey od Ustawy Rady
Nieustaiacey w Roku 1775 az do zaczęcia się Seymu
Ordynaryinego w Roku 1776
Archiwum Sanguszków Sanguszko Archive
1035 Lauda i instrukcje wołyńskie i kijowskie 1778-1790
Warsaw, Poland
Archiwum Glowne Akt Dawnych Chief Archive of Old Acts
Archiwum Komierzowskich Komierzowski Archive
12/12 Korespondencja K.N. Sapiehy
Archiwum Krolestwa Polskiego Archive of the Polish Kingdom
70 Korespondencja do Debolego 1773-1780
89/72 Listy od Stanisława Augusta do Stackelberga 1771-1782
89/85 Korespondencja StanisławaAugusta i Rumiencev 1771-1789
89/91 Myśli króla Stanislawa Augusta
89/93 Table des matières de la partie VIII des memories du Roi
90/10 Entretiens du Roi avec le comte de Stackelberg
262 Korespondencja od Debolego 1779-1781
263 Korespondencja od i do Debolego 1780 do 1789
265 Korespondencja od Debolego 1782-1783
266 Korespondencja do Debolego 1782-1783
267 Korespondencja od Debolego 1785
268 Korespondencja do Debolego 1784-1785
269 Korespondencja od Debolego 1786-1787
378 Korespondencja do Debolego 1787
Archiwum Publiczne Potockich Public Potocki Archive
90 Zbiór pism różnych naleźących do opisu dzieł narodowych od zaczęcia
się Rady Nieustaiącey w Roku 1775 aż do dnia seymu roku 1776 zaczetego.
Zawiera oraz w sobie regestr aktów y sancytów konfederacyi seymu 1776 r.
95/1 Pisma w sprawie Ryxa z Komarzewskim 1785
95/2 Listy polskie z r. 1785
102 Dyaryusz Seymu ordynaryinego warszawskiego Roku 1786 pod laską
marszałka Gadomskiego
279a Korespondencja krajowa z hr. Ignacym Potockim 1783-1779
313/IX-XII Annexy do pamietnikow marszałka Lubomirskiego
Archiwum Radziwillowski Radziwill Archive
V. volume 372. No. 14944 Korespondencja z Stackelbergiem
Warszawa Ekonomiczna
542 Liber Consultationum in Praetorio Civitatis Regio Mtis Antiquae
Varsaviae 1772-1778
Zbiór Popielów
18 Sejm 1786: mowy, protokoły, itd.
25 Sejm 1786 r. Papiery od delegowanych do egzaminowania Rady
Nieustaiącey y Departmentu Woyskowego y Komitetow
28 1779-1782. Protokoły i Relacje Deputacji do Rady Nieustającej
98 Ecrits passés entre le Roi et le Maréchal Rzewuski sur le réforme à faire
et Dépense du Roi. 23 Janvier 1778 - 7 juillet 1779

99 Ecrits passés entre le Roi et le Maréchal Rzewuski en 1778
100 Ecrits passés entre le Roi et le Maréchal Rzewuski en 1777
105 Mowy seymowe 1786 służące do Dyaryusza
125 Acta Seymów 1776, 1778, 1780
126 Acta Seymowe 1782
128 Acta Seymowe 1784
129 Acta Seymowe 15 VIII 1776 do 13 X 1778
130 Acta Seymowe 21 VIII 1780 do 24 XI 1790
131 Acta Seymowe 1 IX 1784 do 20 III 1791
132 Acta Seymowe 1786
133 Acta Seymowe 1786-1791
172 Correspondence éntrangère 1764-1779
210 Korespondencja polska
221 Correspondence éntrangère 1765-1792
235 Zbiór Korespondencji partykularney JK Mci do y od Urodzonych
de Boskamp Lasopolskiego, Everhardtu, Dzieduszyckiego 21 Aprilis 1776
ad 16 Junii 1780.

Paris, France

Archives des Affaires Entrangeres
P 309-314 Poland 1775-1788
T 163 Turkey 1777-1778

London, England

Public Record Office
    State Papers
88 110-15 Poland (including Saxony) 1775-1779
91 90-106 Russia 1775-1780
    Foreign Office
65 1-2 Poland (including Saxony) 1782-1789

PRINTED DOCUMENTARY SOURCES

Anonymous. *Observation d'un Polonois impartial sur l'arrêt rendu à Varsovie le 15 Mars 1785.* Warsaw, 1785.

Archiv der Familie von Stackelberg. Volume I. St. Petersburg, 1898.

Arneth, Alfred (ed.). *Joseph II und Katherina von Russland.* Vienna, 1869.

Catherine II. ''Pismo Ekateriny II k grafu Stakelbergu, 1773-1795 *Russkaia Starina* III:1 (1871), 310-25.

Coxe, William. *Travels into Poland, Russia, Sweden, and Denmark.* 2 volumes. London, 1784.

DYARYUSZ Seymu Ordynaryinego pod związkiem Konfederacyi generalney Oboyga Narodów agituiącego się. Warsaw, 1776.

DYARYUSZ Seymu walnego ordynaryinego warszawskiego sześcio-niedzielnego r. p. 1778 dnia 5 miesiąca października odprawuiącego się. Warsaw, 1779.

DYARYUSZ Seymu wolnego ordynaryinego Warszawskiego sześcio-niedzielnego R.P. 1780 dnia 2 miesiąca października odprawuiącego się. Warsaw, 1780.

DYARYUSZ Seymu wolnego ordynaryinego warszawskiego sześcio-niedzielnego r.p. 1782. Warsaw, 1782.

DYARYUSZ Seymu wolnego ordynaryinego grodzieńskiego sześcio-niedzielnego r.p. 1784 dnia 4 miesiąca października odprawuiącego się. Warsaw, 1784.

Friedrich II. *Politische Correspondenz Friedrichs des Grossen.* Volumes 37-46. Berlin 1896-1939.

Harris, James, Earl of Malmesbury. *Diaries and Correspondence of James Harris.* Volume I. London, 1845.

Joseph II. *Joseph II und Ludwig Cobenzl, Ihr Briefwechsel.* 2 volumes. Vienna, 1901.

Kott, Jan (ed.). *Poezja polskiego oświecenia. Antologia.* Warsaw, 1956.

Ligne, Charles Prince de. *Mémories et mélanges historiques.* Volume I. Paris, 1827.

(Khrapovitskii, Alexander Visilevich). *Dnevnik A.V. Khrapovitskogo.* St. Petersburg, 1874.

Kołłątaj, Hugo. *Stan Oświecenia w Polsce w ostatnich latach panowania Augusta III.* Edited by Jan Hulewicz. Wrocław, 1953.

—————. *Wybór pism politycznych.* Edited by Bogusław Leśnodorski. Wrocław, 1952.

Kraszewski, J.I. (ed.). *Podróz króla Stanisława Augusta do Kaniowa w r. 1787 podług listów Kazimierza Konstantego Hrabiego de Brol Platera.* Wilno, 1860.

Michałowski, Bartłomiej. "Zapiski Mikhalovskogo". *Drevnaia i Novaia Rossaia* XVI, 54-92, 332-71, 552-75, 673-90.

Morawski, Kazimierz Maryan. "Dwie rozmowy Stanisława Augusta z Ksawerym Branickim". *Rocznik Towarzystwa historycko-literackiego w Paryżu, 1868.* Paris, 1869.

Mottaż, Eugeniusz (ed.). *Stanisław Poniatowski i Maurycy Glayre, korespondencya dotycząca rozbiorów Polski.* Translated by Jadwiga Baranowska. 2 volumes. Warsaw, 190.

Naruszewicz, Adam St., *Dyaryusz podróży Nayiaśnieyszego Stanisława Augusta króla Polskiego na Seym Grodzieński zacząwszy od dnia wyiazdu z Warszawy to iest 26 miesiąca Sierpnia Roku 1784 aż do przybycia do Grodna.* Warsaw, 1784.

Naruszewicz, Adam. *Korespondencja Adama Naruszewicza 1769-1792.* Wrocław, 1959.

Naruszewicz, Adam. *Sprawa miedzy Xięciem Adamem Czartoryskim Generałem Ziem Podolskich a Janem Komarzewskim Generałem Majorem przy boku J.K. Mci. i Franciszkiem Ryxem Starostą Piaseczyńskim Kamerdynerem królewskim Oskarżonemi iakoby o zamysł strucia tego xięcia.* Warsaw, 1785.

Niemcewicz, Julian Ursyn. *Pamietniki czasów moich.* 2 volumes. Warsaw. 1957.

Ochocki, J.D. *Pamietnik anegdotyczny z czasów Stanisława Augusta* Posnan, 1867.

Ostrowski, Tomasz. *Poufne więsci z oświeconey Warszawy.* Wrocław 1972.

Pawiński, Adolf (ed.). *Dzieje ziemi kujawskiej oraz akta historyczne* Volume V. Warsaw, 1888.

Poniatowski, Stanisław. "Mémoires du Prince Stanisław Poniatowski". *Revue d'histoire diplomatique* IX (1895), 481-535.

(Potocki, Stanislaw). *Listy polskie pisane w roku 1785 przez Jana Wit.* Warsaw, 1785.

Radziwiłł, Karol Stanisław. *Korespondencja Księcia Karola Stanisława Radziwiłła wojewody wileńskiego, ''panie kochanku'', 1744-1790 z archiwum w Werkach.* Edited by Czesław Jankowski. Cracow, 1898.

Rzewuski, Leon (ed.). *Kronika Podhorecka.* Cracow, 1860.

Sbornik imperatorskogo ruskogo istoricheskogo obshchestva. St. Petersburg, 1767-1916.

Ségur, Louis-Philippe. *Mémoires ou souvenirs et anecdotes.* 2 volumes. Paris, 1841.

Sniadecki, Jan. *Żywot Literacki Hugona Kołłątaja.* Wrocław, 1951.

Stanisław August. ''Listy króla Stanisława Augusta do Szczęsnego Potockiego z lat 1768-1792.'' *Rocznik Towarzystwa Historycko-literackego w Paryżu* III (1871), 259-310.

Stanisław August Poniatwoski. *Mémories du roi Stanislas-Auguste Poniatowski.* 2 volumes. St. Petersburg-Petrograd, 1914-1924.

Stanisław August. *Pamiętniki Stanisława Augusta Poniatowskiego i jego korespondencja z cesarzową Katarzyną II.* Poznań, 1862.

Staszic, Stanisław. *Pisma filozoficzne i spoleczne.* 2 volumes. Cracow, 1954.

Tync, Stanisław (ed.). *Komisja Edukacji narodowej. Wybór źródeł.* Wrocław, 1954.

Vautrin, Hubert. *La Pologne du XVIIIe siècle vue par un précepteur française.* Edited by Maria Cholewo-Flandrin. Paris, 1966.

Volumina Legum czyli przedruk zbioru praw. Volumes XIII-IX. St. Petersburg, 1859-1860.

Wielhorski, Michal. *Essai sur le rétablissement de l'ancienne forme du gouvernement de Pologne suivant la constitution de la République, par le comte Wielhorski, grand-Maitre d'hôtel du Grande Duché de Lithuanie, traduit du Polonais.* London, 1775.

Wybicki, Józef. *Listy patriotyczne.* Edited with Introduction by Kazimierz Opałek. Wrocław, 1955.

——————. *Życle moje.* Cracow, 1927.

Zaleski, Bronislaw (ed.). *Korespondencja krajowa Stanisława Augusta z lat 1784 do 1792.* Poznań, 1872.

Zaleski, Michal. *Pamiętniki Michała Zaleskiego.* Poznań, 1879.

Zbiór praw sądowych na mocy konstytucyi roku 1776 przez JW Andrzeya Zamoyskiego ex-kanclerza, kawalera orła biatego ułozony na seym roku 1778 podany. Warsaw, 1778.

SELECTED SECONDARY SOURCES

Adolphowa, Krystyna. ''Sprawa Kodeksu Zamoyskiego na seymikach litewskich''. *Ksiega pamiątkowa koła historykowsluchaczy Universytetu Stefana Batorego w Wilnie.* Wilno, 1933.

Aragon, Marques d'. *Un Paladin au XVIII siècle.* Paris, 1893.

Askenazy, Szymon. *Przymierze polsko-pruskie.* Warsaw, 1918.

Assorodobraj, Nina. *Początki klasy robotniczej.* Warsaw, 1966.

Bartoszewicz, Julian. *Znakomici mężowie polscy w XVIII wieku.* 3 volumes. St. Petersburg, 1855.

Bernacki, Ludwik. *Teatr, dramat i muzyka za Stanisława Augusta.* 2 volumes. Lwów, 1925.

Bernard, Paul B. *Joseph II and Bavaria.* Hague, 1965.

Bobińska, Celina. *Szkice o ideologach polskiego Oświecenia.* Wrocław. 1952.

——————— , (ed.). *Studia z dziejów wsi małopolskiej w drugiej połowie XVIII wieku.* Warsaw, 1957.

Brandys, Marian. *Nieznany Książe Poniatowski.* Warsaw, 1964.

Broda, Jozef. *Andrzej Zamojski a sprawa chłopska w drugiej połowie XVIII w.* Warsaw, 1951.

Brukner, A.G. "Putashestvye Ektareriny Vtoroi v Krimie". *Istoricheskii Vestnik* XXI (1885), 5-23, 242-64, 444-509.

——————— . "Potushestvye Imperatritsy Ekateriny II w Mogilevie v 1780 godu". *Russkii Vestnik* CLIV, 459-509; CLV, 311-367.

Buczek, Karol. "Z dziejów polskiej archiwistyki prywatney". *Studia historyczne ku czci Stanisława Kutrzeby.* Volume II. Krakow, 1938.

Bystroń, Jan Stanislaw. *Dzieje obyczajów w dawnej Polsce.* 2 volumes. Warsaw, 1960.

Castéra, Jean Henri. *Vie de Catherine II.* 2 volumes. Paris, 1797.

Cérenville. *Memoirs of Prince Potemkin.* London, 1813.

Chamcówna, Mirosława. *Uniwersytet Jagielloński w dobie Komisji Edukacji Narodowej. Szkoła Główna Koronna w latach 1786-1795.* Wrocław, 1959.

——————— . *Uniwersytet Jagiellonski w dobie Komisji Edukacji Narodowej. Szkoła Głowna Koronna w okresie wizyty i rektoratu Hugona Kołłątaja. 1777-1786.* Wrocław, 1957.

Cieślak, Edmund. *Miasto wierne Rzeczypospolitej. Szkice Gdańskie.* Warsaw, 1959.

Ćwik, Wladyslaw. *Miasta królewskie lubelszczyny w drugiej połowie XVIII w.* Lublin, 1968.

David, Curtis C. *Szambelan Jego Królewskiej Mości.* Translated by Teresa Tatarkiewicz. Warsaw, 1967.

Dębicki, Ludwik. *Puławy.* Volume I. Lwów, 1887.

Fabre, Jean. *Stanislaw-Auguste Poniatowski et l'Europe des lumières.* Paris, 1952.

Feldman, Józef. *Na przełomie stosunków polsko-francuskich 1774-1787,* Krakow, 1935.

Ferrand, Antoine François. *Histoire des trois démembrements de la Pologne pour faire suite a l'histoire de l'anarchie de Pologne par Rulhiere.* 3 Volumes. Paris, 1820.

Fisher, Alan W. "Sahin Girey, the Reformer Khan and the Russian Annexation of the Crimea." *Geschichte Osteuropas* XV:3 (September 1967), 341-64.

——————— *The Russian Annexation of the Crimea 1772-1783.* Cambridge, England, 1970.

Geiysztor, Aleksander and others. *History of Poland.* Warsaw, 1968.

Griffiths, David Mark. "Russian Court Politics and the Question of an Expansionist Foreign Policy under Catherine II, 1762-1783." Unpublished Ph.D. dissertation, Cornell University, 1967.

Grochulska, Barbara. "Statystyka ludnościowa Warszawy w drugiej połowie XVIII wieku" *Przegład Historyczny* XIV (1954), 586-608.

Grodzisko, Stanisław. *Obywatelstwo w szlacheckiej Rzeczy-pospolitej.* Kraków, 1963.

Herrmann, Ernst. *Geschichte des russischen Staates.* Volume V. Gotha, 1860.

Horn, D.B. *British Diplomatic Representatives 1689-1789.* London, 1932.

Janik, Michal. *Hugo Kołłątaj.* Lwów, 1913.

Jobert, Ambroise. *La Commission d'Éducation nationale en Pologne.* Paris, 1941.

——————. *Magnats polonais et physiocrates francais (1767-1774).* Paris, 1941.

Kaczmarczyk, Zdzisław and Bogusław Lésnodorski. *Historia państwa i prawa Polski.* Volume II. Warsaw, 1966.

Kalinka, Waleryan. *Ostatnie lata Stanisława Augusta.* 2 volumes. Kraków, 1891.

——————. *Ostatnie lata panowania Stanisława Augusta.* 2 volumes, Poznań, 1868.

——————. *Sejm Czteroletni.* Volume I. Kraków, 1895.

Kalinkiewiczówna, Anna. "Rozkład partii Tyzenhauza na tle sejmików litewskich." *Księga pamiątkowa koła historyków-słuchaczy Uniwersytetu Stefana Batorego w Wilnie.* Wilno, 1933.

Kaplan, Herbert. *The First Partition of Poland.* New York, 1962.

Komarzewski, Jan. *Coup d'oeil rapide sur les causes réeles de la décadence de la Pologne.* Paris, 1807.

Konopczyński, Władysław. *Geneza i ustanowienie Rady nieustającej.* Kraków, 1917.

——————. *Liberum Veto,* Kraków, 1918.

——————. *Polscy pisarze polityczni XVIII wieku* Warsaw, 1966.

——————. *Polska a Turcja.* Warsaw, 1935.

——————. *Stanislaw Konarski.* Warsaw, 1926.

Korzon, Tadeusz. *Wewnętrzne dzieje Polski za Stanisława Augusta 1764-1794.* Volumes I-IV. Kraków and Warsaw, 1897-1898.

Koscialkowski, Stanisław. *Antoni Tyzenhous Studia i szkice przygodne z historii i z jej pogranicza z literaturą.* London, 1956.

——————. "Z literatury polemicznosadowej XVIII weiku." *Ateneum Wilenskie* V:15 (1928), 1-22.

Kostamarov, Kikolai Ivanovich. *Posliedniie gody Riechipospolitei.* St. Petersburg, 1870.

Kowecki, Jerzy, Uniwersal Polaniecki i sprawa jego realizacji, Warsaw, 1957.

Kraszewski, J.I. *Polska w czasie trzech rozbiorów.* 3 volumes. Warsaw, 1902.

Kula, Witold. *Szkice o manufakturach w Polsce XVIII wieku.* 2 volumes. Warsaw, 1956.

Kurdybacha, Lukasz. *Dzieje kodeksu Andrzeja Zamoyskiego.* Warsaw, 1951.

Kutrzeba, Stanislaw. *Historya ustroju Polski w zarysie* 4 volumes. Lwow, 1912.

Łaszewski, Ryszard. *Sejm Polski w latach* 1764-1793, Warsaw 1973.

Łepkowski, Tadeusz. *Polska — Narodziny nowoczesnego narodu.* Warsaw, 1967.

——————. *Przemysł warszawski u progu epoki kapitalistycznej.* Warsaw, 1960.

Lésnodorski, Bogusław. *Dzieło Sejmu Czteroletniego.* Wrocław, 1951. *Polscy Jakobini,* Warsaw, 1960.

Libiszowska, Zofia. *Misja Polska w Londynie w latach 1769-1795.* Łódz, 1966.

Łojek, Jerzy. *Misja Debolego w Petersburgu w latach 1787-1792.* Wrocław, 1962.

Lord, Robert H. *The Second Partition of Poland.* Cambridge, Massachusetts, 1915.

Loret, Maciej. *Kosciół katolicki a Katarzyna II 1772-1782.* Monografie w zakresie Dziejów nowozytnich, Volume 12, Kraków, 1910.

Madariaga, Isabel de. "The Secret Austro-Russian Treaty of 1781". *Slavonic and East European Review* XXXVIII: 90 (December 1959), 114-45.

——————. *Britain, Russia and the Armed Neutrality of 1780.* New Haven, 1962.

Mańkowski, Tadeusz. *Genealogia Sarmatyzmu.* Warsaw, 1946.

Manteuffel, Tadeusz and others. *Historia Polski.* 2 volumes, Warsaw, 1958.

Michalski, Jerzy. "Do dziejow stronnictwa austriackiego i polskiej polityki po I rozbiorze". *Księga pamiątkowa ku uczczeniu siedemdziesiątej rocznicy urodzin prof. dra Janusza Wolińskiego.* Warsaw, 1954.

——————. "Dwie misje księcia Stanisława". *Księga pamiątkowa 150-lecia Archiwum Głównego Akt Dawnych w Warszawie.* Warsaw, 1958.

——————. "Plan Czartoryskich naprawy Rzeczypospolitej" *Kwartalnik Historyczny* LXIII:4 5 (1956), 29-43.

——————. *Polska wobec wojny o sukcesję bawarską.* Warsaw, 1964.

——————. "Sejmiki poselskie 1788 roku" *Kwartalnik Historyczny* LI (1960), 53-73, 331-67, 465-82.

——————. "Sprawa chłopska na sejmie 1773-1775". *Przegląd Historyczny* XLV (1954), 31-13.

——————. "Sprawa dysydencka a zagadnienia gospodarcze w opinii publicznej w pierwszych latach panowania Stanisława Augusta". *Przegląd Historyczny* XL (1949), 156-63.

——————. "Sprawa miejska w opinii szlacheckiej przed Sejmem Czteroletnim". *Przegląd Historyczny* XLII (1951), 291-303.

——————. "Zagadnienie polityki antycechowej w czasach Stanisława Augusta". *Przegląd Historyczny* XLV (1954), 639-47.

Morawski, Kazimierz. "Do charakterystyki okresu Rady nieustającej i genezy przymierza polsko-pruskiego". *Kwartalnik Historyczny* XXVII (1913), 316-35.

——————. *Ignacy Potocki.* Volume 21 of Monografie w zakresie dziejów nowożytnych. Kraków, 1911.

——————. "Pogląd na opozycję magnacka między pierwszym rozbiorem a sejmem czteroletnim". *Studia historyczne wydane ku czci Prof. Wincentego Zakrzewskiego.* Kraków, 1908.

——————. "Prokonsulat Stackelberga". *Biblioteka Warszawska* LXXI:2 (1911), 560-68.

Mrozowska, Kamilla. *Szkoła Rycerska Stanisława Augusta Poniatowskiego.* Wrocław, 1961.

Nadzieja, Jadwiga. *Generał Józef Zajączek od Kamieńca do Pragi 1752-1794.* Warsaw, 1964.

Nanke, Czesław. *Szlachta wołyńska wobec konstytucji trzeciego maja.* Lwów, 1907.

Nowak, Juliusz. *Satyra Polityczna Sejmu Czteroletniego.* Kraków, 1933.

Nowak, Tadeusz, and Jan Wimmer. *Dzieje oręża polskiego.* Volume I. Warsaw, 1968.

Olszewski, Henryk. *Sejm rzeczypospolitej epoki oligarchii.* Poznań, 1966.

Opałek, Kazimierz. *Prawo natury u polskich fizjokratów.* Warsaw, 1953.

Polski Słownik Biograficzny. Kraków 1936-ongoing.

Radwański, Zbigniew. *Prawa kardynalne w Polsce.* Poznań, 1952.

Rose, William J. *Stanislas Konarski.* London, 1929.

Rostworowski, Emanuel. "Ksiądz pleban Kołłątaj". *Wiek Dziewiętnasty. Prace ofiarowane Stafanowi Kieniewiczowi w 60 rocznicę urodzin.* Warsaw, 1967.

——————. "Hugo Kołłątaj wobec zagadnienia obywatelskiej siły zbrójnej". *Przegląd Historyczny* XLII (1951), 331-64.

——————. "La Suisse et la Pologne au XVIIIe siècle". *Echanges entre la Pologne et la Suisse.* Geneva 1964.

——————. *Legendy i fakty XVIII wieku.* Warsaw, 1966.

——————. *Ostatni król Rzeczypospolitej.* Warsaw, 1966.

——————. "Reforma Pawłowska Pawła Ksawerego Brzostowskiego (1767-1795)" *Przegląd Historyczny* XLIV: 1-2 (1953), 101-52.

——————. *Sprawa aukcji wojska na tle sytuacji politycznej przed sejmem czteroletnim.* Warsaw, 1957.

——————. "Z dziejów genezy Targowicy". *Przegląd Historyczny* XLV:1 (1954), 14-35.

Rudnicki, Kazimierz. *Biskup Kajetan Sołtyk.* Volume 5 in Monografie w zakresie dziejów nowożytnych. Kraków, 1906.

Rymszyna, Maria. *Gabinet Stanisława Augusta.* Warsaw, 1962.

Szcząska, Zbigniew. "Sąd sejmowy w okresie Rady Nieustającej. Proces Barona Juliusa." *Przegląd Historyczny* LXII (1971):3, 421-36.

Schmitt, Henryk. *Dzieje Polski.* Volume III. Lwów, 1888.

Semkowicz, Władysław. *Przewodnik po zbiorze rekopisów wilanowskich.* Warsaw, 1961.

Sidorowicz, W. "Walka o moskiewski alians". *Polityka Narodow* VIII:3 (1936), 256-82.

Smoleński, Wladyslaw. "Przyczyny upadku projektu Kodeksu Zamoyskiego". *Pisma Historyczne.* Volume I. Krakow, 1901.

Soloviev, S.M. *Istoria Padeniia Polshi.* Moscow, 1863.

——————. *Istoria Rosii s dreevnieshikh vremen.* Volume XV. Moscow, 1960.

Wilder, Jan Antoni. *Traktat handlowy polsko-pruski z roku 1775..* Warsaw, 1937.

Zahorski, Andrzej. *Centralne Instytucje Policyjne w Polsie w dobie rozbiorow.* Warsaw (1959).

Zajączkowski, Andrej. *Główne elementy kultury szlacheckiej w Polsce. Ideologia a struktury spoleczne.* Wrocław, 1961.

Zieńkowska, Krystyna. *Jacek Jezierski, Kasztelan łukowski 1722-1805.* Warsaw, 1963.

INDEX

4